Measuring Human Rights

The measurement of human rights has long been debated within the various academic disciplines that focus on human rights, as well as within the larger international community of practitioners. Written by leading experts in the field, this is the most up-to-date and comprehensive book on how to measure human rights.

The book:

- draws explicitly on the international law of human rights to derive the content of human rights that ought to be measured
- contains a comprehensive methodological framework for operationalizing this human rights content into human rights measures
- includes separate chapters on the methods, strengths and biases of different human rights measures, including events-based, standards-based, survey-based, and socio-economic and administrative statistics
- covers measures of civil, political, economic, social and cultural rights
- includes a complete bibliography, as well as sources and locations for data sets useful for the measurement of human rights.

This volume offers a significant and timely addition to the field, and will be of interest to academics and NGOs, INGOs, international governmental organizations, international financial institutions, and national governments themselves.

Todd Landman is Professor in the Department of Government and a Member of the Human Rights Centre at the University of Essex. He is author of many books, including *Studying Human Rights* (2006), *Protecting Human Rights* (2005), and *Issues and Methods in Comparative Politics* (2000, 2003, and 2008).

Edzia Carvalho is currently researching her PhD on public health policy in India in the Department of Government at the University of Essex. She has an MA in Human Rights (Essex 2006), and an MA in International Relations (Mumbai 2003).

Measuring Human Rights

Todd Landman and Edzia Carvalho

Routledge
Taylor & Francis Group

LONDON AND NEW YORK

First published 2010 by Routledge
2 Park Square, Milton Park, Abingdon, Oxon, OX14 4RN
Simultaneously published in the USA and Canada
by Routledge
270 Madison Avenue, New York, NY 10016

Routledge is an imprint of the Taylor & Francis Group, an informa business

Typeset in Times New Roman by
Taylor & Francis Books

British Library Cataloguing in Publication Data
A catalogue record for this book is available from the British Library

Library of Congress Cataloging in Publication Data
Landman, Todd.
 Measuring human rights / Todd Landman and Edzia Carvalho.
  p. cm.
 Includes bibliographical references.
 1. Human rights. 2. Human rights monitoring. I. Carvalho, Edzia. II.
Title.
 JC571.L246 2009
 323.072'3–dc22
                          2009016179

ISBN 978-0-415-44649-5 (hbk)
ISBN 978-0-415-44650-1 (pbk)
ISBN 978-0-203-86759-4 (ebk)

Contents

Illustrations

Figures

Tables

Boxes

Acknowledgements

Over the years, the two of us have been involved in a variety of international events and activities relating to human rights measurement and assessment all over the world. These events have taken us throughout Europe and North America, and as far afield as Mongolia (at least from our Essex base anyway!). There are many people to whom we would like to extend our thanks and heartfelt appreciation for their intellectual input, hard work, and dedication to the development and improvement of human rights measures.

Outside the University of Essex, we would like to extend our thanks to Patrick Ball, David Cingranelli, David Richards, Joe Foweraker, Mark Gibney, Ronald Francisco, Reed Wood, Bethany Barratt, Shareen Hertel, Rajeev Malhotra, Ken Mease, Joachim Nahem, Meghna Abraham, Julia Häusermann, Ingrid Wetterqvist, Matthew Sudders, Tsetsenbileg Tseven, Stuart Weir, David Beetham, Christian Davenport, Steve Poe, Neil Mitchell, Sabine Carey, Eric Neumayer, Oona Hathaway, Daniel Manrique, David Sulmont, Javier Pereira, Nicholas Fasel, the Rights and Equity Team at the UK Department for International Development (DFID), and John Osbourne.

At Essex, we have had the privilege to work and interact with members of the Human Rights Centre and the Department of Government who have in many ways contributed to our thinking about human rights and measurement issues, including Paul Hunt, Aida Paskeviciute, Kevin Boyle, Nigel Rodley, Geoff Gilbert, Françoise Hampson, John Bartle, Thomas Scotto, David Sanders, Thomas Plümper and Vera Troeger.

Todd Landman would like to express his personal thanks to his closest friends and family, without whom survival through the many ups and downs of the writing process would not have been possible. In particular, thanks to Oliver Heginbotham, Sophia Laura Landman and Briony Rose Landman for making his home such a fun, adventurous and lively environment in which to ponder life's bigger questions. Warm thanks and affection to Melissa Landman for providing such a firm foundation and an inspiration for life's many challenges. Deep thanks go to Pavlenka and Stephen Small for providing so much support, and special thanks to Roni and Laraine Shachnaey for their commitment, friendship and spirit throughout the last couple of years.

Finally, Todd Landman would like to thank Edzia for her commitment to a number of projects, not least of which this one. Throughout her time at Essex, Edzia has been an unbelievable asset to the Department and the Human Rights Centre and has worked tirelessly, efficiently and with great attention to detail on a wide range of challenging endeavours while continuing to pursue her PhD.

Edzia Carvalho would like to thank Todd Landman for his generosity, kindness and compassion as a mentor and a friend. It has been an honour and a blessing to share in his vision of contributing to the theory and practice of human rights. Deepest thanks to Prof. Peter Ronald deSouza and colleagues at Lokniti (Centre for the Study of Developing Societies, Delhi) for their unwavering guidance and encouragement over the years. No words or actions would ever be enough to repay the debt owed to them. Thanks to friends from the 'Essex human rights mafia' all over the world who continue to inspire as examples in courage and commitment. Heartfelt thanks to friends and family in India, especially Dina and Clifford Da Silva, Sr. Aradhana A.C., Vishaka Sridhar, Praful Auti, Banasmita Bora, Solano Da Silva, Rama Murkunde, V. SriRanjani, Sanjeevini Badigar, Zinia Martires and Elvira D'Souza who have been unshakeable in their faith and endless sources of joy.

At Essex, deepest thanks to Fr. Martin Boland, Przemyslaw Piatkowski, Chih Mao Tang, Natascha Warta Neudorfer, Kai Yin Low, Joo-Young Lee, Melissa D'Mello and Andrea Ruggeri for being such good company through the long silences. Warmest thanks to Samuel Mansell for his gentleness, kindness and constant reminders of the wonders of smiling. Finally, to her parents, Zino and Edna Carvalho, Edzia would like to extend her deepest gratitude and humblest thanks for being her reason for everything.

Todd Landman and Edzia Carvalho
Colchester, Essex

1   Introduction

This book is about measuring human rights. Its point of departure is that human rights have become an accepted legal and normative standard through which to judge the quality of human dignity as it is experienced by over five billion people around the world in a multitude of very different social, economic and political contexts. The standard has arisen through the concerted efforts of thousands of people over many years inspired by a simple set of ideas that have become codified through the mechanism of public international law and realized through the domestic legal frameworks and governmental institutions of states around the world. However, this realization is incomplete, where there remains a large and variable gap between the expectations for human dignity outlined through human rights standards and the reality of the precariousness of those rights as they are variously enjoyed around the world. Both the standard and the gap are subject to measurement, where we understand measurement to be the cognitive process through which abstract concepts find numerical expression in the form of valid, reliable and meaningful indicators. This book does not concern itself with the ongoing and unresolved debates about the absence of agreed philosophical foundations for human rights, nor does it engage with the persistent arguments based on cultural relativism. Rather, it takes for granted that the extant international law of human rights is both a useful starting point for the measurement of human rights and the outcome of a long and iterated negotiated settlement across many diverse state and non-state actors about what constitutes the basic guarantees for the realization of human dignity.

Moreover, the book is committed to developing new and reviewing the many different existing ways in which measurement can capture the lived empirical experience of human rights in order that scholars and practitioners can conduct the best systematic analysis of human rights problems and puzzles around the world. It recognizes that the lived experiences of human rights are not always known to the observer, but in following the tradition of the social sciences and statistics, it argues that methods for measurement and analysis can use samples of information about the known patterns in the human rights experience to make inferences about those that are not known. As the book shows, careful attention to the source materials, bias, error, coding of the source

material and other significant methodological concerns can equip human rights
analysts with the necessary tools to capture and analyse in systematic fashion
significant human rights problems in ways that will lead to their enhanced
protection in the future.

We thus see this book as grounded in a particularly *pragmatic* approach on
the functions and dimensions of human rights that have provided important
starting points for their measurement. The remainder of this chapter provides
a background to the development of human rights measurement, the different
functions and uses for it, a brief overview of the different types of human rights
measures and an outline of the rest of the chapters in the book. We believe that
this book represents an important milestone in the ongoing development of
human rights measurement in particular, and in the struggle for human rights in
general, since the best way to understand problems is to measure them, analyse
them and provide solutions to them.

Background developments

The measurement and monitoring of human rights has been a mainstay activity
of human rights non-governmental organizations (NGOs) primarily for
advocacy purposes and since the 1980s has become increasingly important for
a wide range of human rights scholars and practitioners working across the
broad spectrum of human rights issue areas from many different disciplinary
perspectives. Human rights NGOs such as Amnesty International and Human
Rights Watch use monitoring systems to track the degree to which international human rights treaties have been implemented, to alert the international
community about egregious violations of human rights, to mobilize different
constituencies around particular human rights issues and to advocate for additional standard setting in the international law of human rights. The discipline
of political science has arguably had the largest impact on the development
and analysis of human rights measures, which has been complemented and,
in some instances, surpassed by cutting-edge work in the NGO sector. Since
the behavioural revolution in the social sciences in the 1930s and 1940s, political
science has sought to measure and analyse political *violence* from state and
non-state actors, an effort that has since the 1980s turned to systematic analysis of the *causes and consequences of cross-national variation in human rights
protection around the world* (e.g. McCamant 1981; Mitchell and McCormick
1988; and Landman 2005a). Complementing these developments, scholars have
published collections and reviews of human rights measures produced by academics and non-governmental organizations (Claude 1976; Jabine and Claude
1992) and efforts to collate and assess the quality of human rights measures
continue to be carried out (e.g. see Green 2001; Landman and Häusermann
2003; Landman 2004, 2006, 2009).

Since the publication of *Human Rights and Statistics* (Jabine and Claude
1992), there have been an increasing number of efforts to measure *more* and
different categories of human rights (e.g. the Cingranelli and Richards

Human Rights Data Project at www.humanrightsdata.com), and there have been a variety of international conferences and workshops on human rights measurement sponsored by professional academic organizations (e.g. the 2004 Chicago workshop organized by the Human Rights Section of the American Political Science Association and the 2005 conference on economic and social rights organized by the Human Rights Institute at the University of Connecticut) and international organizations (e.g. the 2000 conference on human rights and statistics in Montreux, followed by similar summits in ensuing years in Merida, Munich and Brussels). The most recent and cutting-edge advances in human rights measurement have come from the non-governmental sector, especially those organizations working with truth commissions around the world. In particular, the work of the Human Rights Data Analysis Group (HRDAG) at the American Association for the Advancement of Science in Washington, DC (and now the Benetech Initiative in Palo Alto, California) has been instrumental in developing systematic techniques for the measurement and analysis of large-scale human rights violations across a range of different country contexts, most notably Peru, Colombia and East Timor (see Ball et al. 2003; Guzmán et al. 2007; Silva and Ball 2007).

The increasing provision and availability of human rights measures has led to a new demand within the international human rights and donor communities, such as the United Nations (UN), the World Bank, and the aid ministries in the US (USAID), UK (DFID), Sweden (SIDA), Canada (CIDA) and Denmark (DANIDA) to integrate human rights assessment into overall policy formulation and aid allocation strategies. Donors such as DFID in the UK use human rights assessment in their aid programming to find ways in which different aid modalities can address particular needs within partner countries to improve the human rights situation, while at the same time address larger questions of poverty reduction. In contrast, the Millennium Challenge Account uses human rights measures as an incentive to allocate aid to those countries that can demonstrate improvements in their human rights performance. In addition, the Office of the High Commissioner for Human Rights (OHCHR) in Geneva has been engaged in a long-term process of consultation with international experts to provide matrices of human rights indicators for use in state party reports to the treaty monitoring bodies, while the United Nations Development Programme's (UNDP) Oslo Governance Centre has produced guides on measures of good governance and human rights for use in their own country offices, as well as across the donor community more generally (see UNDP 2004, 2006).

Taken together, there is clearly a need for greater clarity about and attention to the measurement of human rights, while demand for human rights measures is unlikely to subside any time soon. This present volume is the first book-length treatment of the topic since the publication in 1992 of *Human Rights and Statistics: Getting the Record Straight* (Jabine and Claude 1992) and, therefore, represents a significant stocktaking and synthesis of the developments in this important field of work. We believe that our effort offers a number of distinct advantages that move the debate on measurement forward. First, it presents an assessment and analysis with one authorial voice rather than a collection of chapters collated by a set of editors. We have thus been able to draw together the burgeoning literature on human rights measurement and provide a synthesis in ways that have not yet been done. Second, it draws explicitly on the extant international law of human rights to derive the content of human rights that ought to be measured and therefore attempts to establish a stronger foundation and justification for the measurement strategies we cover. Third, it contains a comprehensive methodological framework for operationalizing this human rights content into human rights measures, which draws on larger debates about measurement in the social sciences. Fourth, it has separate chapters on the methods, strengths and weaknesses of events-based, standards-based and survey-based measures, as well as socio-economic and administrative statistics. Fifth, it covers measures of civil, political, social, economic and cultural rights, while recognizing the many challenges that remain for their measurement. Finally, in addition to standard bibliographic references, the book also includes lists of sources and locations for extant data sets useful for the measurement of human rights.

The purpose of measuring human rights

Human rights measures serve a variety of important and inter-related functions across the academic and non-academic sectors of the human rights community, including:

1 Contextual description and documentation
2 Classification
3 Monitoring
4 Mapping and pattern recognition
5 Secondary analysis and policy prescription
6 Advocacy and political dialogue

Contextual description and documentation provide the raw information for monitoring carried out primarily by non-governmental organizations, as well as for developing and deriving standardized measures of human rights. Measures will include locally-based and rich descriptive statistics covering human rights violations, conditions and perceptions, as well as the activities of state and non-state actors that have a bearing on human rights. Many human rights organizations offer annual reports on different regions, countries and human rights issues, all of which use in some degree different types of human rights measures. Second, *classification* allows for the differentiation of rights violations across their different categories and dimensions, and for grouping states and regimes into different categories. Such a move is one level above pure descriptive analysis and begins to group observations about human rights together into 'classes' of things that can then be compared and analysed (see Landman 2000, 2002, 2003, 2008).

Third, human rights measures can be used for *monitoring* the degree to which states respect, protect and fulfil the various rights set out in the different treaties to which they may be a party. Such monitoring is typically done over time, where the availability of human rights measures increases the possibility of making larger analytical statements about the changing human rights situation within a particular region, country, part of a country, or for particular groups of people, such as migrants, ethnic minorities, women, the poor, etc. For example, the OHCHR has been working on detailed matrices of human rights indicators that can be used for state party reporting to the various UN treaty monitoring bodies, while human rights measures seem particularly apt for state party reporting under the new Universal Periodic Review (UPR) process in the Human Rights Council.

Fourth, measures can be used for *mapping and pattern recognition*, where time-series and spatial information on the broad patterns of violations within and across different countries can be compared (e.g. human rights performance within less-developed countries). Fifth, and related to the fourth function, human rights measures are essential for *secondary analysis*, which is carried out by social scientists such as hypothesis-testing, prediction and impact assessment; the inferences from which can be fed into the policy making process. Typical social science analysis uses human rights measures to test for the significance of relationships between and among human rights and other variables, such as democratic institutions, levels of economic growth and inequality, the involvement in domestic and international conflict, and a range of other relevant variables that may account for the variation in the protection of human rights (Landman 2005a, 2006a: 93–106). Findings that are upheld statistically in the presence of control variables and other tests can then lead to the formulation of policy responses dedicated to improving human rights. In addition, such secondary analysis can be used to examine the degree to which a particular policy intervention has had a direct or contributory effect on a particular human rights problem (see Landman 2006a: 126–39)

Finally, human rights measures can serve as *important advocacy tools* at the domestic and international level by showing the improvement or deterioration in rights practices around the world. Human rights organizations and intergovernmental organizations with a mandate to work on human rights use human rights measures to press for change in particular regions and countries, while international donor agencies and donor countries increasingly see human rights measures as a crucial aspect of their work in analysing areas of government performance that can be improved or areas of governance that are in need of foreign assistance through the extension of aid and other support (see Chapter 3 in this volume). Moreover, the accumulation of information on human rights protection in the world and the results of systematic analysis can serve as the basis for the continued development of human rights policy, advocacy, education and political dialogue, as more and more indicators, results of different kinds of analyses and research outputs enter the public domain (Rubin and Newberg 1980: 268; Claude and Jabine 1992: 5–34).

These different purposes for human rights measurement, while significant enterprises in and of themselves, should not be seen as mutually exclusive. Rather, they should be seen as progressive and cumulative, effectively building from one to the next to provide a complete process of assessment and analysis. For example, an advocacy project that wants to demonstrate the presence of ethnic discrimination in the access to adequate healthcare and to advocate for the necessary legal and policy reforms will necessarily engage in many of these different functions of measurement. The advocacy element of the project would necessarily rely on the results of some form of secondary analysis of health statistics, which is predicated on the collection, monitoring and mapping of these statistics. In this way, what appears to be a simple advocacy project, can actually involve quite extensive use of the different functions of measurement outlined here.

Overview of the book

With this background and preliminary look at how human rights measures are used, we can now introduce the main structure of the book and highlight the essential contributions of each chapter. We have made every attempt to organize the book in a way that each chapter builds on the previous chapters with a fair degree of cross-referencing within the text and comparisons between the strengths and weaknesses of different measures. The process of social science measurement comprises a series of common methodological components, such as source material, sampling, coding, reliability tests and analysis, while the measures themselves provide different ways of capturing in quantitative fashion the many categories and dimensions of human rights. There is, thus, a common set of concerns addressed in each chapter while the many differences of each kind of measure are discussed at length. These concerns and discussions are complemented throughout with examples from existing work on measuring and analysing human rights from the academic and non-academic sectors.

To begin our exposition of different methods for measuring human rights, Chapter 2 shows how the substantive content of human rights has evolved since the promulgation of the 1948 Universal Declaration of Human Rights. The chapter follows the development of international human rights law, including the main instruments, General Comments and debates surrounding the interpretation of human rights from the larger academic, non-governmental and policy communities. The framework of content that we present moves well beyond the 'generations' approaches to human rights or any privileging of particular rights, to show that human rights now comprise a set of categories (i.e. civil, political, economic, social and cultural), which have different dimensions grounded in the notion of state obligations to respect, protect and fulfil. In this way, we argue that all rights comprise a negative obligation of states to refrain from violating rights and to prevent third parties from doing the same, as well as a positive obligation of states to provide the necessary resources for fulfilling their rights commitments. This means that measures for human rights will necessarily include those that capture their *violation* and their *realization*, which we group into the notions of rights in principle (i.e. those formal legal commitments that states make), rights in practice (i.e. the enjoyment of rights by individuals on their own or as members of a group), and rights as policy (i.e. the structures, processes and outcomes of governmental efforts to promote and protect human rights). This framework also includes reference to a series of organizing and human rights *principles* that deepen the understanding of implementation of human rights and the processes involved in their realization. These principles include availability, accessibility, adaptability and accept-ability in reference to the implementation of human rights policies, and non-discrimination, participation, progressive realization and effective remedy in the processes involved in human rights policies.

The framework for the substantive content of human rights developed in Chapter 2 is then taken as the starting point for what Chapter 3 calls the 'moment of measurement', which comprises a series of levels or steps that draw on the seminal work on social science measurement developed by Adcock and Collier (2001) in the *American Political Science Review*. These levels include the *background concept* (human rights), the *systematized concept* (the content of particular human rights), the development of *indicators* (the mea-sures that feature throughout the book), and the actual assigning of *scores on units* (e.g. countries, sub-national units and individuals). The chapter argues that many existing human rights measures have gone through these different levels to varying degrees and then outlines the different types of measures that have been developed over the past few decades. These types of measures include *events-based* (i.e. counting violations or human rights related events), *standards-based* (i.e. coding narrative human rights reports into comparable scales), *survey-based* (i.e. individual-level data on perceptions of or experi-ences with human rights), and *socio-economic and administrative statistics* that capture different elements of the policy process. The chapter concludes by arguing that there are multiple measures that capture the various dimensions of the different human rights delineated in our framework.

Chapters 4 through 7 then discuss in depth the assumptions, genesis, devel-opment, use, strengths and weaknesses of each type of human rights measure. Chapter 4 shows how events-based measures of human rights draw on the larger tradition of events analysis in the social scientific work on political violence. The development of this kind of measure has been undertaken pri-marily by non-governmental organizations, in particular the American Asso-ciation for the Advancement of Science and Benetech, in which the 'who did what to whom' model has been developed to deconstruct human rights events into their constitutive parts and quantified in ways that have proved vital for human rights analysis in truth commissions and international criminal tribu-nals. Chapter 5 shows how standards-based measures code source material on human rights conditions within countries to provide comparable data for cross-national and time-series data sets, which have then been used for mapping, monitoring and analysing the cross-national variation in the protection of particular sets of human rights. Chapter 6 moves the discussion on to the use of survey methods for capturing individual perceptions of human rights conditions or experiences of human rights violations in ways that utilize the inferential capacity of random samples for depicting human rights conditions for whole countries, or for particular groups of people within countries. Again, the development of survey-based measures has been pursued primarily by the non-governmental sector, in particular by Physicians for Human Rights. Chapter 7 completes our discussion of different types of measures by reviewing the various ways in which socio-economic and administrative statistics can be used as important 'proxy' measures for the different dimensions of human rights, including the state obligations to respect, protect and fulfil.

Finally, Chapter 8 concludes the book by reviewing the many achievements that have been made in the development of measures for human rights. The fact that a second book is needed in this issue area to capture the many positive developments is evidence alone that this is a burgeoning field in the study of human rights. However, despite the many achievements in the generation and provision of different types of human rights measures, there is still much work to be done. The review of measures shows that many parts of the framework that we develop in Chapter 2 remain virtually empty, where more attention has been dedicated to the development of measures for the 'respect' dimension of civil and political rights and the 'fulfil' dimension of economic and social rights. There is, thus, a need to develop measures for the 'fulfil' and 'protect' dimensions of civil and political rights, and the 'respect' and 'protect' dimensions for economic and social rights. This suggests that much work is needed on examining how measures can capture third-party violations of civil and political rights and how they can capture the efforts that governments are making to fulfil their civil and political rights commitments.

It also suggests that much more work is needed on developing 'violations' approaches to economic and social rights by both the state and by third parties; an area that is in need of urgent attention, as many governments have turned to the private sector for the provision of social and economic welfare. The chapter argues further that continued attention is needed to the fundamental issues of social science measurement, including the types and number of source materials, the potential for bias and error at every stage of the measurement process, and the importance of accountability and transparency of the measurement process itself. Inattention to these issues can lead to 'overconfident, and therefore, irresponsible' use of measures in the analysis of significant human rights problems (see Hoover et al. 2009: 1). We only hope that this book contains the necessary critical analysis of the state of the art on human rights measurement and that it can begin to make a difference for the future of this exciting field.

2 The content of human rights

Introduction

Scholars and practitioners of human rights will recognize the difficulty in bringing about consensus across academic disciplines and global and local communities on the exact content of human rights. Do human rights refer solely to those rights recognized in international human rights law or domestic law? Are they moral claims that individuals can make against the state even when they are not recognized legally? Are human rights a 'discourse' (or multiple discourses) employed by individuals and groups – local, global and transnational – to gain attention for or legitimize their claims or a 'language' used by states to pursue national security and economic interests?

This book takes the view that human rights are moral claims accorded legal recognition and states are legally obliged to ensure that they respect, protect and fulfil these claims. Human rights are 'political norms dealing mainly with how people should be treated by their governments and institutions' (Nickel 2006). These norms have become entrenched within international politics and, arguably, validate (or have been used to justify) the legitimacy of domestic regimes and the pursuit of national interests (Landman 2005a). By delineating the purely legal conception of human rights from its philosophical and socio-anthropological perspectives, this book attempts to provide scholars and practitioners in the field a secure (although partial) basis from which to commence the task of monitoring and measurement.

This chapter highlights the meaning of human rights as conceived in international law and the interpretations of these rights by institutions set up to monitor the implementation of the law by states. This is accompanied by a brief sketch of the international human rights mechanisms that are involved in standard setting and implementation. The chapter then maps out the content of human rights and draws attention to the principles, categories and dimensions as derived from the international law of human rights. These features are particularly important for measurement as they can be used to assess whether the legislation, policies and practices of states fulfil their international and domestic legal obligations. Individuals and human rights monitoring organizations can hold states to account for their acts of commission or omission in discharging these obligations. The final section of the chapter examines some measurement models that have been conceptualized to facilitate the assessment of states' performance in the protection of these rights. By comparing frameworks of human rights measurement as developed from international law, the chapter assesses the key trade-off between complexity, validity and viability that arises in the application of these measures.

The international human rights regime

The 'terrain of human rights' is quite vast and far-reaching given the involvement of institutions and individuals at the international and local levels in the making of laws and policies, their implementation and enforcement. The six distinct organizational fields of relevance to human rights include institutions that are directly involved in these processes (public international and domestic organizations) as well as those that have an indirect impact on them ('not for profit' international and domestic organizations) (Landman 2006a; see Table 2.1). These organizations have been said to constitute 'the international human rights regime' (Donnelly 1986; Beetham 1999; Montgomery 1999; Moravcsik 2000; Nowak 2003). A third set of organizations may also affect human rights protection and implementation of human rights standards; these 'for profit' organizations at the international and domestic levels of functioning may be involved in standard setting and implementation. It could be argued that these organizations are not part of the human rights regime, but influence it and are influenced by it (Alston 2005; Clapham 2006). However, since the formal regime is concerned with the setting and realization of international human rights standards, this section of the chapter restricts itself to outlining those mechanisms developed at the international, regional and domestic levels since the advent of the 1948 Universal Declaration that engage in these tasks.

Human rights, as expressed in international law, are 'specific norms that emerged from a political project' that commenced in the aftermath of the First World War and gained traction as an immediate consequence of the Second World War (Nickel 2007: 7). The Charter of the United Nations thus endorsed the existence and necessity of human rights; however, it is not the foundation for these norms (Freeman 2002). The international human rights regime, like other international regimes, is a 'deliberately constructed, partial international order' consisting primarily of states, which establishes a set of norms (in this case, human rights) that prescribe the behaviour of those states that become members of the regime (Hasenclever et al. 2000: 3). Unlike other regimes, however, this particular set of mechanisms does not seek to regulate inter-state policies and behaviour; rather, it focuses on holding governments accountable for their policies and practices that affect their citizens. International human rights norms are made by states to be implemented within each territorial jurisdiction by these states. The regime is wholly centred on ensuring the protection of human dignity by states. This goal of regulating state behaviour

Table 2.1 The organizational fields of human rights

	Sphere of Activity		
	Public	*Private Not for Profit*	*For Profit*
Primary levels of activity	*I*	*II*	*III*
International	International governmental organizations (IGOs): United Nations (UN) European Union (EU) Council of Europe (CoE) Organization for Security and Cooperation in Europe (OSCE) North Atlantic Treaty Organization (NATO) Organization of American States (OAS) African Union (AU) International Criminal Court (ICC) Organization of Petroleum Exporting Countries (OPEC) Organization for Economic Cooperation and Development (OECD) International Bank for Reconstruction and Development (IBRD) International Monetary Fund (IMF) World Trade Organization (WTO)	International non-governmental organizations (INGOs): Amnesty International Anti-Slavery International Article 19 Human Rights First Human Rights Watch International Federation of Human Rights Leagues International Service for Human Rights Minority Rights Group Penal Reform International World Organization Against Torture Transnational advocacy networks (TANs)	Multinational corporations (MNCs): Shell Nike Reebok British Petroleum Mitsubishi Mitsui Siemens Du Pont General Motors Sumitomo Ford Motor Toyota Exxon Commercial banks and securities firms: Citicorp Merrill Lynch JP Morgan Morgan Stanley UBS Investment Bank
	IV	*V*	*VI*
Domestic	Independent nation-state governments Sub-national governments (state, municipal, local) Public schools	Non-governmental organizations (NGOs) Civil society organizations (CSOs) Social movement organizations (SMOs) Warlords/ guerilla movements/'uncivil' movements/death squads	Domestic business firms Commercials banks Private schools Private armies/ mercenary firms

Source: Landman, 2006a: 21

towards what have been otherwise considered matters internal to the state, challenges the concept of state sovereignty, which has served as one of the key foundations for realist theory in international relations and classical international law (Moravcsik 2000; Landman 2005b).

The international human rights regime comprises formal institutions (UN and regional bodies) and informal ones (non-governmental organizations), which are involved in the processes of standard setting (through which moral norms have the force of law when incorporated into international and regional multilateral treaties), monitoring and enforcement, and impact and influence each other (Beetham 1999; Nowak 2003; Landman 2006a). Beginning with the Universal Declaration of Human Rights (UDHR) in 1948 (see Box 2.1), the UN has developed the majority of the international human rights standards that exist today, and has created a system of institutions to implement these standards and monitor their achievement. These institutions include treaty bodies, charter bodies and specialized agencies, which contribute to the work of standard setting, implementation and monitoring. It is obvious that the authority of the UN in the field of human rights derives from the maze of international commitments that have been developed under its wing and to which its member states have consented. With the call for the 'mainstreaming of human rights' within the UN and its agencies, the UN remains unparalleled as the organizational focal point for developing legal human rights norms and striving towards the maintenance and effectiveness of the human rights regime at the international and regional level (UNGA 2005).

Box 2.1 The Universal Declaration of Human Rights – 'the moral anchor of a worldwide movement'

'All human beings are born free and equal in dignity and rights. They are endowed with reason and conscience and should act towards one another in a spirit of brotherhood.'

Article 1, *Universal Declaration of Human Rights*, 1948

The Universal Declaration of Human Rights adopted by the United Nations General Assembly in 1948 reflected the need for 'a new humanistic legal order' to create and maintain conditions that would enable people everywhere to live lives of dignity. The Declaration reflects the *four freedoms* formulated by US President F. D. Roosevelt in 1941 – freedom of expression, freedom of faith, freedom from want and freedom from fear. The Preamble to this Declaration calls it 'a common standard of achievement', obligating governments to create, at the minimum, conditions for the enjoyment of a set of basic rights (Alfredsson and Eide 1999; Baehr et al. 1999). The Declaration arose as an immediate consequence of the 'collective moral repulsion' towards the atrocities committed during the

Second World War and the Holocaust; however, it is essentially rooted in 'a shared consciousness of vulnerability' reflected in the innumerable historic human struggles to alleviate suffering and uphold human dignity (Lauren 1998; Alfredsson and Eide 1999; An-Na'im 1999; Waltz 2002). It was the product of an 'international political movement with aspirations to create [an] international law' of human rights. (Nickel 2007: 7).

The text of the Declaration was drafted by the Human Rights Commission and its sub-committees and then adopted by 48 countries (with eight abstentions) that constituted the United Nations. Articles 1 and 2 represent the core principles of the Declaration – the inherent equality of all individuals and the freedom that they enjoy by virtue of being human. The rights included in the Declaration could be classified as follows: security rights (or 'personal integrity rights'), due process rights, political rights, social rights and equality rights (Nickel 2006). Many of the rights included in the Declaration were subsequently incorporated within the two international covenants – on civil and political rights, and on economic, social and cultural rights, and the treaties on specific rights or particular vulnerable groups.

Persistent and stringent criticisms of the Declaration have been voiced since its adoption. Doubts were raised about the applicability of the principles enshrined within, given the political nature of the drafting exercise. The Human Rights Commission sought to bypass this problem of foundations, which has been dealt with elsewhere in this chapter, by focusing on the creation of 'norms' and forging international consensus on their application. However, the concept of human rights is drawn from the same mould as the Lockean concept of natural rights; it is widely regarded as rooted in the Western liberal tradition of the primacy of individual liberty over collective freedoms and of rights over responsibilities (Freeman 2002; Donnelly 2007; Nickel 2007). Consequently, concerns were also raised regarding the universal applicability of the Declaration, for example, whether it was relevant to people living in so-called 'Islamic countries', or other regions of the world where the focus on individual rights was tempered by the rights of groups as well (An-Na'im 1999; Higgins 1999). Other critics highlighted the compromises that were negotiated during the drafting process of the Declaration to ensure the co-operation of the major powers and which resulted in what was considered to be a philosophically ambiguous document that was silent on some important issues of the day like colonialism and imperialism. The fact that the Declaration wasn't legally binding on states was of most concern to advocates and critics alike. As a set of standards for all states to aspire to, the Declaration did not create or reiterate the responsibilities of states in international law (Alfredsson and Eide 1999; Freeman 2002). Critics of the exercise remained sceptical of the reach of the Declaration stating that it was unrealistic to expect states to allow international interference in what they would consider matters solely within a state's jurisdiction.

Advocates of the Declaration argue that it has been an innovative and revolutionary document, the spark that lit the way for the emergence of a global human rights movement. It brought into existence a 'self-contained, comprehensive system of rights' that radically altered the relationship between states and their citizens at the national level and between states as sovereign autonomous members of the international community (Alfredsson and Eide 1999: xxx). It spurred the development of the international law of human rights with over 200 international human rights instruments, considered to be universal standards to measure the performance and even the legitimacy of governments, as well as creating international legal obligations on states to respect, protect, promote and fulfil human rights (Baehr et al. 1999; Freeman 2002). National courts and regional and international organizations cite the Declaration as one of the moral sources for recognizing human rights (Hannum 1998; Montgomery 1999). Recent research has also sought to place into proper perspective the role of small states in the drafting and adoption of the Declaration, thus debunking the notion that it was irrevocably influenced by big power politics. In fact, it has been argued that the non-binding nature of the Declaration was ultimately helpful, as it was useful in persuading, rather than coercing, states to accept and adhere to the principles and rights enshrined within (Morsink 1999; Waltz 2002).

Sixty years since the adoption of the Declaration, while the recognition of human rights and reporting of their violations has exponentially increased, transnational efforts to stem the ever-growing tide of human rights abuses needs to be strengthened further. The Declaration is an internationally recognized instrument that has provided activists and practitioners with the moral, political and legal arguments necessary to protect rights in countries where human rights are not recognized or protected by states. It has undoubtedly become 'the moral anchor of a worldwide movement' (Morsink 1999: xii).

At the regional level, most regional intergovernmental organizations have been involved in the development and implementation of human rights treaties. Three regions of the world – Europe, the Americas and Africa – have set up human rights regimes with human rights standards and associated institutions. Europe has three regional mechanisms – the Council of Europe (COE), the European Union (EU) and the Organization for Security and Co-operation in Europe (OSCE) – which together form an intricate, elaborate and expanding system of human rights protection in the region. The European Convention on Human Rights adopted in 1950 under the aegis of the COE provides individuals with the right to appeal to the European Court of Human Rights once legal remedies are exhausted in their domestic jurisdiction. The OSCE has additional institutions that monitor different dimensions of human rights in Europe, while the EU has a variety of policy instruments for the promotion of human rights, the most important of which include the Copenhagen criteria for membership of the EU. The Inter-American system created by the Organization of American States stands second only to the European system in terms of its spread and effectiveness, with a body of law made by and applicable to the states parties to the 1969 American Convention on Human Rights, and is the only system that allows for *in situ* visits by personnel from the regime to investigate human rights conditions. The third regional human rights system is in Africa under the auspices of the African Union. It was established by the African Charter on Human and Peoples' Rights in 1979 and was implemented by a Commission of experts. Recent developments in the region include the establishment of an African Court of Human and People's Rights in 2006 to address individual complaints on violations of the Charter by state parties. While efforts to develop a regional human rights system in Asia are in their infancy, the League of Arab States has made considerable progress in the development of a regional system, with the adoption of the 2004 Arab Charter on Human Rights, which came into force in 2008.

These human rights regimes at the international and regional levels have weak enforcement mechanisms and implementation processes, which ultimately depend on states to meet their legal obligations in good faith (*pacta sunt servanda*). States are expected to submit periodic reports on their progress to the respective monitoring mechanisms, but penalties do not exist should states fall behind in their reporting. In some cases, like the Optional Protocol 1 to the International Covenant on Civil and Political Rights (ICCPR) or the Optional Protocol to the International Covenant in Economic, Social and Cultural Rights (ICESCR), states may agree to let citizens file individual petitions on alleged violations before the international treaty body; however, these mechanisms have no means available to enforce their decisions and are dependent on states to accept and implement their instructions (Steiner and Alston 1996; Symonides 2003; Donnelly 2007a).

Working in tandem with this set of institutions comprised primarily of states and institutional arrangements established to regulate the behaviour of states is, the informal human rights regime made up primarily of international and domestic non-governmental organizations (NGOs). NGOs provide increasing assistance to states to establish, develop and monitor international regimes (Beetham 1999; Landman 2005b, 2006a; Donnelly 2007a). International NGOs (INGOs) have played an active role in standard setting, monitoring and mobilizing for human rights causes around the globe (see Risse et al. 1999; Welch 2001; Bob 2005). For example, the role of Amnesty International and the International Commission of Jurists in drafting the UDHR and the UN

Convention against Torture (CAT) cannot go without mention (Clark 2001; Huckerby and Rodley 2009). NGOs also have an important role in monitoring and implementing the human rights regime, more so because of the weak enforcement mechanisms of the UN and most regional systems. They are considered to be the link between the domestic and international levels of the human rights regime; through the formation of 'transnational advocacy networks' they put pressure on states to change their human rights behaviour and adopt and 'internalize' human rights norms (Keck and Sikkink 1998; Boli et al. 1999; Risse et al. 1999). Together, the formal and informal elements of these different human rights regimes contribute to the standard setting, implementation and monitoring of human rights obligations of states.

Human rights in international law

The content of human rights as established in international law is dependent on the creation and adoption of legal standards by states; norms that enable the human rights community to hold states accountable for those actions that violate the dignity of individuals residing within their jurisdictions. Human rights standards have been the unique contribution made by international law to the discourse on human rights. However, these standards comprise only the substantive portion of the concept. Human rights also include procedural or 'process' features, which are those facets of the concept that states need to consider when implementing the standards that they have accepted. This section of the chapter discusses the features of human rights as elaborated in international law and the interpretations of the law by international human rights treaty bodies and special mechanisms. It also addresses one of the most controversial debates that arose at the time of the drafting of the two International Covenants in the 1950s and 1960s – the creation of 'categories' of human rights. Human rights create obligations on states for their fulfilment. The nature of these obligations has also been debated under the notion of 'dimensions', which is also tied into the controversy related to the categories of rights. This section thus formulates a comprehensive model of human rights in international law and briefly sketches the literature on the various elements that comprise the concept of human rights as interpreted by the institutions involved in standard setting, implementation and monitoring at the international level.

The content of human rights

As a prelude to the discussion on the constitutive elements of human rights, this section takes a step back to understand what is meant by a 'concept' in the general sense of the term and the manner in which the meaning and measurement of concepts are inextricably linked. There are at least two interrelated views on this issue: the semantic approach, which focuses on the definition of a concept as the primary and only source of meaning, and the causal ontological approach, which maintains that a concept comprises both the 'theoretical and empirical analysis of [an] object or phenomenon referred to by the word' (Goertz 2006: 3–4). This book adheres to the latter approach and attempts to highlight human rights as a specific theoretical and empirical concept. This exercise has important implications for the measures used to monitor human rights (which are elaborated in subsequent chapters) and the conclusions that are derived from the results.

A concept can be understood as being multilevel and multidimensional in character. There are essentially three levels at which a concept can be mapped: a) the 'basic level', which consists of the theoretical propositions about the core meaning of the concept; b) the 'secondary level', which highlights the constitutive elements of the concept; and c) the 'indicator/data level', which operationalizes these elements into specific measures (Goertz 2006: 4–6, 30–65).[1] Human rights, at Goertz's basic level, are conceptualized as minimum legal standards accepted by states that a) ensure the protection of the dignity of individuals, b) define the limits of state behaviour towards their residents and c) can be used to hold states accountable for the failure to meet these standards (Chapman and Russell 2002; Sepúlveda 2003; Nickel 2007). These rights have been distinguished into three 'categories': a) civil and political rights, b) economic, social and cultural rights, and c) solidarity rights. This classification of rights has attracted considerable debate, with one group making the claim that these three categories create distinct and separate obligations on states for the provision of rights; on the other hand, scholars have taken the stand that while the core content of each human right is distinct and separate, the obligations it creates on states for its implementation and monitoring are similar to those brought about by other human rights. This issue is addressed later in the chapter.

The concept of human rights can be delineated into three 'secondary level' concepts: 'rights-in principle', 'rights-in-practice' and 'rights-as-policy' (see Figure 2.1 and Landman 2002).[2] Rights measured in principle evaluate the international and national commitments made by states (*de jure* state compliance). Rights in principle are the necessary condition among these three dimensions at the secondary level of the concept; without the creation and acceptance of legal standards by states, human rights would exist (depending on the foundational theories of rights) at the moral plane of existence, but they could not be justiciable by law. However, legal protections of rights are not sufficient conditions for the existence of human rights; by accepting these obligations, states agree to execute policies that ensure the implementation of the provisions of these treaties. Hence, rights measured as policy outcomes assess the impact of government policies on the enjoyment of rights. Rights measured in practice determine the actual enjoyment of rights by individuals and groups in states (*de facto* state compliance) (Landman and Häusermann 2003; Landman 2004, 2006b). Each of these three 'dimensions' has indicators that have been used to clarify the content of the concept further and are discussed in the subsequent paragraphs.[3]

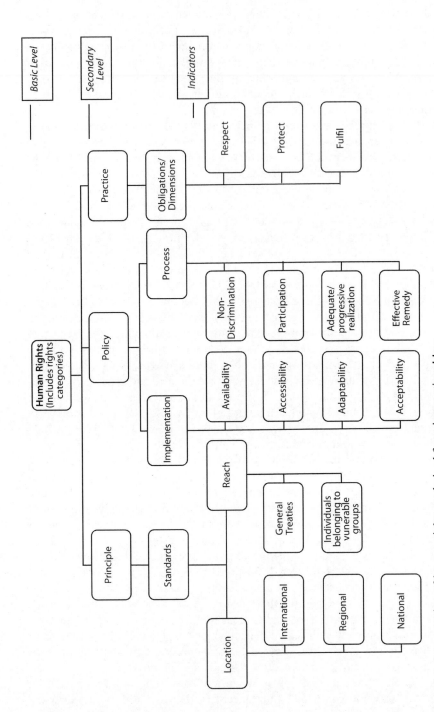

Figure 2.1 A conception of human rights as derived from international law

Sources: CESCR 1999a; UNDP 2000; Green 2001; Sepúlveda 2003; Landman 2004; Goertz 2006

Rights in principle

Human rights standards are those specific rights that have been codified in international law. When a state signs or accedes to an international treaty, it formally accepts a legally binding obligation to implement the provisions of the treaty. These standards have been adopted at the international, regional and national levels (see the discussion above). They have also taken the form of two types of documents: a) a treaty or declaration protecting human rights in general and b) the protection of the rights of individuals who are members of specific groups (see Table 2.2).

The International Bill of Rights – the 1948 Universal Declaration of Human Rights, the 1966 International Covenant on Civil and Political Rights and the 1966 International Covenant on Economic, Social and Cultural Rights – and subsequent treaties such as the 1984 Convention against Torture highlight the legal protections that individuals can claim from the state.[4] The two Covenants also reflect the most commonly accepted categorization of human rights: a) civil and political rights, b) economic, social and cultural rights, and c) solidarity rights. Civil and political rights protect the person-hood of individuals and their ability to participate in the public activities of their countries; economic, social and cultural rights provide individuals with access to economic resources, social opportunities for growth and the enjoyment of their distinct ways of life, as well as protection from the arbitrary loss of these rights; and solidarity rights seek to guarantee for individuals access to public goods like development and the environment (Freeman 2002; Landman 2006a). This categorization loosely follows a temporal frame; it has been suggested that since human rights are the consequence of struggles of peoples against oppression and injustice, successive generations of people have fought for distinct 'generations of rights', with civil and political rights comprising the first generation, economic, social and cultural rights making up the second generation, and solidarity rights being the third. Consequently, it was suggested that civil and political rights are preeminent and should be attained before the struggles for the other rights could be pursued (Rich 2002). This division of human rights has been challenged by scholars in the community. Art. 1 of the UDHR states that 'all human beings are … equal in dignity and rights'. It should follow that the rights that they enjoy are also equal. The 1993 Vienna Declaration and Programme of Action states that human rights are indivisible, interrelated and interdependent. The enjoyment and implementation of one set of rights is inextricably linked to the fulfilment of the other rights (Boyle 1995; Alfredsson and Eide 1999; Donnelly 1999; Freeman 2002).

The second set of human rights treaties protects the rights of individuals who by virtue of being members of a particular group or possessing certain characteristics, may be particularly vulnerable to rights violations. Thus, the 1966 International Convention on the Elimination of all Forms of Racial Discrimination (CERD) addresses all forms of racial discrimination, the 1989

Table 2.2 List of human rights protected under international law

1	Non-discrimination	30	Trade unions
2	Life	31	Rest, leisure and paid holidays
3	Liberty and security of the person	32	Adequate standard of living
4	Protection against slavery and servitude	33	Education
5	Protection against torture	34	Participation in cultural life
6	Legal personality	35	Self-determination
7	Equal protection of the law	36	Protection of and assistance to children
8	Legal remedy	37	Freedom from hunger
9	Protection against arbitrary arrest, detention or exile	38	Health
10	Access to independent and impartial tribunal	39	Asylum
11	Presumption of innocence	40	Property
12	Protection against *ex post facto* laws	41	Compulsory primary education
13	Privacy, family, home and correspondence	42	Humane treatment when deprived of liberty
14	Freedom of movement and residence	43	Protection against imprisonment for debt
15	Nationality	44	Expulsion of aliens only by law
16	Marry and found a family	45	Prohibition of war propaganda and incitement to discrimination
17	Protection and assistance of families	46	Minority culture
18	Marriage only with free consent of spouses	47	No imprisonment for breach of civil obligations
19	Equal rights of men and women in marriage	48	Protection of children
20	Freedom of thought, conscience and religion	49	Access to public service
21	Freedom of opinion and expression	50	Democracy
22	Freedom of the press	51	Participation in cultural and scientific life
23	Freedom of assembly	52	Protection of intellectual property rights
24	Freedom of association	53	International and social order for realizing rights
25	Participation in government	54	Political self-determination
26	Social security	55	Economic self-determination
27	Work	56	Women's rights
28	No compulsory or forced labour	57	Prohibition of the death penalty
29	Just and favourable conditions of work	58	Prohibition of apartheid

Sources: Davidson 1993: Appendix 1; Gibson 1996: 37–38; Green 2001: 1069; Donnelly 2003: 24
Reproduced from Landman, 2006a: 16

Convention on the Rights of the Child (CRC) specifies the legal protections to be given to the rights of children and the obligations accrued to the state to uphold these rights, and the 1979 Convention on the Elimination of Discrimination against Women (CEDAW) highlights the rights of women and ensures them protection from discrimination on arbitrary or unjustified grounds. Other rights protections have been provided to individuals with disabilities, to those who belong to an indigenous or ethnic population, and to migrant workers.

Rights in policy

The formal human rights regime establishes two types of institutional mechanisms to oversee the implementation of the treaties. The treaty bodies allow for the creation of committees of experts to which state parties report periodically on the progress in the protection and promotion of human rights, and which in some cases adjudicate individual complaints against state parties over the breach of their treaty obligations. There are eight international human rights treaty bodies and similar committees established by the regional human rights treaties, which are primarily responsible for the monitoring of the treaty concerned. Additionally, the treaty bodies led by the Committee on Civil and Political Rights (CCPR) and the Committee on Economic, Social and Cultural Rights (CESCR) have taken the lead in clarifying the meaning of the rights, the nature of state parties' obligations under the treaty, as well as the specific principles and procedures involved in implementing these obligations by drafting 'General Comments' or 'General Recommendations' (see, for example, CCPR 1989, 2004; CESCR 1990, 2000; CRC 2003).

The UN Economic and Social Council (ECOSOC) has created the office of the UN Human Rights Council (formerly the UN Commission on Human Rights), an intergovernmental group of representatives whose functions include investigating and addressing instances of violations of human rights. The Commission has established the Special Procedures, which are assigned mandates for investigation of human rights violations in particular countries or violations of specific rights. The special procedures differ from the treaty body procedures because, unlike the latter, which apply only to those states that have ratified the relevant treaties, the special procedures are applicable to all states. These procedures consist of experts in the field who often take the initiative in clarifying the scope and content of the human right they are monitoring. For example, the Special Rapporteur on the Right to the Highest Attainable Standard of Health has contributed to further clarifying the meaning of the right to health in his annual reports to the UN Commission of Human Rights and the UN General Assembly (Rosas and Scheinin 2001; Hunt 2003a, 2003b, 2004a, 2004b, 2005, 2006, 2007, 2008; Rodley 2003; Symonides 2003).

The human rights mechanisms also provide guidance to states on the protection and promotion of human rights by elaborating on a set of human rights principles. They concern the manner of implementing policies for the enjoyment of human rights: non-discrimination, participation, adequate progress and effective remedy.[5] These were envisioned with regard to all human rights guaranteed by the international human rights covenants and treaties (UNDP 2000: 93–95). The principle of non-discrimination has been repeatedly enshrined in international law, beginning with the International Bill of Rights (UDHR, Art. 2; ICCPR, Art. 2; ICESCR, Art. 2 (2)) and in the subsequent conventions on rights of individuals belonging to vulnerable groups, as well as the treaties setting up the regional human rights systems. This principle seeks to ensure that individuals are not discriminated against except on the basis of justifiable legal criteria which are reasonable and objective (CCPR 1989; Hunt et al. 2002). Participation in decision-making is a principle that has also been protected in international law (see, for example, UDHR, Art. 21; ICCPR, Art. 25) through participation in the political process and in the making of decisions that have an impact on the enjoyment of the other rights. This principle includes availability and access to information, freedom to use this information and the provision of opportunities to participate in the policy-making process (CCPR 1996; UNDP 2000; Conte 2004).

The third human rights principle, i.e. adequate progress, is related to the concepts of 'progressive realization' subject to the use of the maximum resources available which are included in Art. 2 (1) of the ICESCR and, which some scholars argue, is applicable only to the rights included in this treaty. This is recognition of the fact that resources available to states are limited and they need to be spent on priority areas determined by the state, but informed by the state's human rights obligations. Rights that impose an immediate obligation towards realization are the substantive economic, social and cultural rights such as the rights to food, health, housing, education and work. General or basic obligations towards the rights to non-discrimination, legal remedies and effective participation are also of an immediate nature and not subject to progressive realization (CESCR 1990; UNDP 2000; Green 2001; Chapman and Russell 2002; Sepúlveda 2002; van Bueren 2002). Civil and political rights are considered to impose the obligation towards immediate realization. This distinction between immediate and progressive realization has been challenged by recent developments in law and its interpretation (Eide 2001; CRC 2003; Chapman 2007). For example, Donnelly (2007b: 48–50) suggests with the support of empirical examples that all human rights go through a process of development which reaches a minimal level of achievement in the institutionalization of these norms. The fulfilment of rights, is an ongoing recursive process that is contingent on existing socio-political and economic circumstances. The final principle to be used for process indicators is effective remedy, which ensures redress through judicial, quasi-judicial, administrative and/or informal mechanisms when rights are violated. This principle also has been included in international treaties (UDHR, Arts 8, 9, 10; ICCPR, Art. 2 (3)) and various provisions in the ICESCR have been interpreted to include justiciability of the rights enshrined therein (see CESCR 1990; UNDP 2000; CCPR 2004).

In addition to the human rights principles mentioned above, a set of 'organizing principles' – availability, accessibility, acceptability and adaptability – have also been elaborated by the CESCR as guidelines for states to implement the rights to food, education and health.[6] Availability refers to the resources and infrastructure required for the functioning of the programmes that states provide as a fulfilment of their obligations. It refers to the implementation of policies that ensure that the core content of the right is made available to all individuals. Accessibility requires that provisions for implementing the right make the enjoyment of the right within reach of all individuals. This principle comprises non-discrimination in access, physical accessibility (with regard to safety and convenience) and economic accessibility (affordability). Acceptability consists of the relevance, cultural appropriateness and quality of the resource being provided. States are obligated to ensure that the provision of rights is in keeping with cultural and local sensibilities. The fourth principle, i.e. adaptability, refers to flexibility in the implementation of policies to ensure that these adapt to the changing needs of societies and communities (CESCR 1999a, 1999b, 2000). These indicators are related to the concept of progressive realization of rights. It may be argued that most rights cannot be immediately secured by states, but call for prioritization; socio-economic and political conditions and limited resources at the disposal of states determine the making and execution of policies. If we accept this premise, then the indicators that measure the gradual implementation of policies using a human rights-based approach would be applicable to all categories of rights.

Rights in practice

The last concept that would help explain the meaning of human rights has been conceptualized as the 'dimensions' of human rights. This notion of dimensions has evolved from capturing the temporal evolution of rights to highlighting the precise nature of the legal obligations of states, and the policy and practical implications of fulfilling these commitments. Civil and political rights were often considered to be 'negative rights' as their implementation supposedly required the state to simply refrain from interfering in their enjoyment. Economic, social, cultural and solidarity rights, on the other hand, were referred to as 'positive rights' as their implementation was thought to require investment of limited state resources for their enjoyment. These distinctions present a 'false dichotomy' between the categories of rights. All rights have positive and negative characteristics, with the state being obligated to desist from actively preventing the enjoyment of rights, as well as to put into place policies to facilitate their pursuit. This has been reiterated by the CCPR and the CESCR (CESCR 1990; Holmes 1999; CCPR 2004; UNDP 2006; Donnelly 2007b).

The dimensions of rights have since been reconceptualized along the lines of an 'obligations' approach, which relates to the obligations that states are bound to uphold as parties to international treaties and covenants (Eide 1989; Sepúlveda 2003; Chapman 2007). The obligations of states to respect, protect and fulfil rights were originally thought of with respect to the rights in the UNCESCR and applied by the CESCR to the rights to adequate food, education and health (CESCR 1999a, 1999b, 2000). The United Nations Development Programme (UNDP) then adapted this framework to specify states' obligations towards all human rights, an application that was later recognized by the CCPR (CESCR 1999b: para. 15; UNDP 2000; CCPR 2004). The obligation to respect rights entails refraining from actively depriving people of a guaranteed right. This requires that states parties not to deny or limit access to the enjoyment of rights and desist from a policy of direct or indirect discrimination. The obligation to protect rights involves preventing other actors – individuals, groups or corporations – from depriving people of a guaranteed right. Finally, the obligation to fulfil rights refers to working actively to ensure through the creation of systems of governance, the provision of resources and infrastructure to allow all individuals to enjoy the rights guaranteed to them under international law. This obligation would expect that the state execute policies that, for example, eliminate discrimination based on sex or race in the workplace, or provide access to primary and higher education to economically deprived or socially excluded sections of the population (UNDP 2000; Green 2001; Sepúlveda 2003; Landman 2006b).

Measurement complexity, validity and viability

The conception of human rights as derived from international law was outlined in the preceding section of the chapter. This concept consists of three constitutive elements: standards that determine the limits of state behaviour towards its residents and its obligations to enable the enjoyment of their rights (i.e. rights in principle); the policies that are implemented to realize these rights (i.e. rights as policy); and the actual realization of the three dimensions of these rights (i.e. rights in practice). Each of these constitutive elements is further divided into a set of indicators as a tangible measure of an abstract concept. However, like any other concept in the social sciences, human rights has attracted complex and contested meanings; the intricate latticework of concepts that constitute human rights have often led to problems of validity and viability in developing measures for monitoring human rights. What do we measure when we measure human rights? Do indicators used to measure the concept do the job? Can viable human rights measures – indicators that do not consume financial and human resources and are easily available and accessible – also be valid? This section of the chapter presents four pathways that have been suggested to address this trade-off between the complexity, validity and viability of measurement:

1   The 'basic rights' argument – the list of rights protected in international law can be reduced to a select set of rights to be used as proxy measures for the others;
2   The 'obligations' argument – at a minimum, human rights measures should reflect the *de facto* protection of rights in a state;
3   The 'implementation' argument – human rights measures should reflect the claim that human rights are concerned with the process of achieving rights and not just their outcome; and
4   The 'unique rights' argument – each right enshrines a distinct obligation that is not reducible to a general set of principles; therefore, each human right needs to be modelled separately and distinctly from other rights.

The 'basic rights' argument

The notion of 'basic rights' might be traced back to the Lockean conception of natural rights to life, liberty and property. In more recent times, it has been argued that the list of rights that were set out in the UDHR and subsequently protected by the two Covenants and regional treaties could be reduced, for a variety of reasons, to a 'short-list' (Donnelly and Howard 1988: 214). These vary from Shue's set of three rights (security, subsistence and liberty rights, mirroring Locke), Donnelly and Howard's (1988) list of ten rights grouped into four clusters (survival rights, membership rights, protection rights and empowerment rights), and Nickel's (2007) identification of seven families of rights (security rights, due process rights, liberty rights, rights of political participation, equality rights, social rights and rights of distinctive groups). If we accept the idea that rights are interdependent, then Donnelly and Howard (1988) suggest that a set of rights could be selected as complementary to the rights enshrined in the UDHR. These scholars have presented a theoretically substantiated argument for this exercise in reduction, thus ensuring that indicators used to measure these rights would be valid and the conclusions drawn from the results of the assessment could be generalized to the broader family of rights. Moreover, narrowing down the list of rights to be monitored by states would be viable, since it would enable the freeing up of limited resources and significantly diminish the complexity in measurement of human rights (Donnelly and Howard 1988; Shue 1996; Nickel 2007: 92–103). Following this suggestion might reduce the breadth of rights to be monitored; however, the complexity of the measurement (suggested by the conceptual model mapped out in Figure 2.1) remains untouched.

The 'obligations' argument

This alternative is an attempt to reduce the complexity of rights measurement while attempting to retain the validity of the measures used and making the process of measurement a viable one. Since the international law of human rights creates obligations on states to respect, protect and fulfil rights, it would be essential to map at least this *de facto* enjoyment of rights. Landman (2006b) combines this 'obligations' approach with the classification of categories and suggests a simple 2 × 3 framework of measurement of rights (see Figure 2.2). Undoubtedly, developing indicators and monitoring the protection of rights using this framework is not resource intensive. The framework is easy to understand and apply (see UNDP 2000: 102; Landman 2006b). However, the inherent simplicity of this alternative might present the temptation to measure outcomes without adequate disaggregation to capture elements of non-discrimination. The lack of indicators on the process of implementation raises questions about the validity of the measures used (see relevant discussion in Chapter 7 in this volume).

The 'implementation' argument

Since human rights are concerned with the process of achieving rights and not just their outcome, measuring the implementation of policies drawn up for the

Dimensions of human rights

		Respect No interference in the exercise of the right	Protect Prevent violations from third parties	Fulfil Provision of resources and the outcomes of policies
Categories of human rights	Civil and political	1 Torture, extra-judicial killings, disappearances, arbitrary detention, unfair trials, electoral intimidation, disenfranchisement.	2 Measures to prevent non-state actors such as militias, uncivil movements, or private sector firms and organisations.	3 Investment in judiciaries, prisons, police forces, electoral authorities, and resource allocations to ability.
	Economic, social, and cultural	4 Ethnic, racial, gender, or linguistic discrimination in health, education, and welfare, and resource allocations below ability.	5 Measures to prevent non-state actors from engaging in discriminatory behaviour that limits access to services and conditions.	6 Progressive realisation Investment in health, education and welfare, and resource allocations to ability.

Figure 2.2 Categories and dimensions of human rights
Source: Landman 2006b: 5

enjoyment of human rights would be an essential part of measuring rights. One such framework incorporates the constitutive elements of the conceptual model mapped out earlier in this chapter and applies this to the right to the highest attainable standard of health (see Table 2.3). This example includes specific indicators on the policy process. Input indicators that are included here measure the investment and expenditure of state resources to establish institutions, infrastructure, programmes, etc. to implement a right. Process indicators measure the implementation of policies and provisions at the different stages. Performance indicators map the time taken to produce the various outputs pre-determined by the policies and programmes. Output indicators measure the immediate results of a particular policy. Outcome indicators map the long-term impact of a policy or programme as well as the overall enjoyment of a right (UNDP 2002; Landman and Häusermann 2003; Shrestha and Oiron 2006). While this framework of indicators might be valid, i.e. they measure rights as opposed to the outcome of the enjoyment of rights, the trade-off here has clearly been with the issue of complexity and validity.

The 'unique rights' argument

The fourth and final alternative to addressing the trade-off between the complexity, validity and viability of rights measures is the argument that each human right is unique in the claims that individuals enjoy and the obligations to which states accede. Consequently, a general conceptual model of human rights is not applicable. Each human right would be measured using a distinct framework mapping the meaning of the right as protected in international law. This would be based on the interpretation of the right published by treaty

Table 2.3 Assessing state's children's rights obligations using the child's right to health as an example

a) Obligations of states towards the child's right to health

Obligations of states	Availability					Accessibility			Adaptability (to the evolving capacities of the child)	Acceptability (best interests of the child being paramount)
	Input (state resources invested; legislation & policies approved)	Process (functioning of different aspects of policies & provisions)	Performance (time taken to produce output)	Output (immediate results)	Outcome (survival & devt as min. outcome)	Non-discrimination	Physical	Economic		
Respect rights (by state)	Including right to health in devtal* projects as policy determinant	Including right to health at every stage of implementing devtal projects	Time taken to complete devtal projects after excluding potential violations of right to health	No. of devtal policies that include right to health as policy determinant	Short- & long-term health effects of including right to health in devtal projects	Devtal projects that violate the right to health of particular sections of the population	Devtal projects that impede physical access to health services	Devtal projects that reduce economic access to health services	Do state policies on developmental projects allow for increased participation of older children?	Do developmental projects violate best interests of the child with regards to its right to health?
Protect rights (from violation by non-state actors)	Legislation/ policies on detecting industrial pollution	Including right to health at every stage of implementing industrial projects	Economic costs of excluding potential violations of right to health	No. of industrial projects that include right to health as policy determinant	Levels of industrial pollution that impact the child's right to health	Industrial projects that violate the right to health of particular sections of the population	Industrial projects that impede physical access to health services	Industrial projects that reduce economic access to health services	Do state policies on industrial projects allow for increased participation of older children?	Do state policies on industrial pollution protect the child's right to health?
Fulfil rights (promote and facilitate by the state)	Budgetary allocation & spending on child immunization	No. of doctors trained to administer child immunization	Time it takes to immunize children in a district	No. of children immunized in a year	Fatality rate for children immunized for a disease	Do all children have access to immunization services irrespective of social inequalities?	Distance between immunization centre & nearby villages	Cost to travel to immunization centre if immunization is free	Do state health policies that allow for increased participation of older children?	Do state immunization policies promote best interests of the child?

Note:

* - 'devt' is the abbreviated form of 'development' and 'devtal' is the abbreviated form of 'developmental'.

Sources: CESCR, 1999; UNDP, 2000: 102; Green, 2001: 1074; Landman, 2004.
Reproduced from Carvalho 2008: 551–552.

b) Obligations of States to adhere to human rights principles when providing for the child's right to health

Human rights principles	Availability					Accessibility			Adaptability (to the evolving capacities of the child)	Acceptability (best interests of the child being paramount)
	Input (State resources invested; legislation & policies approved)	Process (functioning of different aspects of policies & provisions)	Performance (time taken to produce output)	Output (immediate results)	Outcome (survival & devt* as min. general outcome)	Non-discrimination	Physical	Economic		
Participation (meaningful and effective)	Budgetary allocation & spending on health education (linked to right to information)	No of teachers provided training in health education	Time it takes to educate children about common diseases, first aid, etc.	No of children provided health education in a year	Level of awareness among children about common diseases, first aid, etc.	Do all children have access to health education irrespective of social inequalities?	Distance between village and centre providing health education	Cost to travel to centre providing health education	Do state health education policies provide for children's participation?	Do state health education policies promote the best interests of the child?
Effective remedy (judicial, quasi-judicial and/or informal)	Legislation/ policies on remedies available to children on violation of right to health	No of judges and lawyers trained on the child's right to health	Time it takes to train judges & lawyers on the child's right to health	Levels of awareness among judges and lawyers on the child's right to health	Cases on the violation of the child's right to health admitted in court	Do all children have access to judicial remedy on violation of the right to health?	Distance between nearest judicial tribunal and village	Cost to invoke judicial remedies on the violation of right to health	Do remedial mechanisms provide for children's participation?	Do remedial mechanisms for violation of the right to health promote best interests of the child?
Adequate progress in realisation (benchmarks & targets)	For budgetary allocation & spending on health services	For no. of doctors that should be trained to administer child immunization	For time it should take to immunize children in a district	For no. of children that should be immunized in a year	For fatality rate for children immunized for a disease	For no. of children who have access to immunization services irrespective of social inequalities	For avg. proposed distance between immunization centre & nearby villages	For proposed cost to travel to immunization centre if immunization is free	For increased participation of older children	For state immunization policies that promote best interests of the child

Note:
* - 'devt' is the abbreviated form of 'development'.

Sources: CESCR, 1999; UNDP, 2000: 102; Green, 2001: 1074; Landman, 2004.
Reproduced from Carvalho 2008: 551–552.

bodies and special procedures, which clarify the nature of the obligations of states with respect to the right and the process to be followed to implement the provisions of the treaty with respect to that right. One such example is the work of the Special Rapporteur on the Right to the Highest Attainable Standard of Health and the researchers who have assisted him in clarifying the meaning of the right to health and developing indicators to measure its implementation (see Hunt 2003a, 2006; Backman et al. 2008). Like the previous alternative, the measures adopted here are valid but complex and not viable for states to develop and use.

The four alternative pathways discussed above reflect efforts to address the trade-off between the complexity and viability of human rights measurement, while attempting to produce valid measures for the purpose. Table 2.4 summarizes these relationships and highlights various measures that have been used to monitor human rights. We suggest that there is a direct and negative relationship between measurement complexity and viability. The adoption of a complex conceptual framework for measurement might reduce its viability (with respect to financial costs, and the availability and accessibility of the data required). The validity of the measures used is determined by the conceptual model of human rights suggested in Figure 2.1. Human rights measures could either be employed to map the complete conceptual framework of human rights or certain constitutive elements. This choice has a related impact (which may be negative or positive) on measurement viability. Subsequent chapters in this volume will highlight specific measures that have been used to measure human rights. These are events-based measures (Chapter 4), standards-based measures (Chapter 5), survey-based measures (Chapter 6), and official socio-economic and administrative statistics (Chapter 7). These measures have been used variously in each of the alternative pathways discussed above. Survey-based measures and official statistics have been employed as measures in all four pathways, while events-based measures and standards-based measures have been utilized in some of these alternatives. The choice of pathway

Table 2.4 Trade-off between measurement complexity, validity, and viability

Alternative	Complexity	Viability	Validity	Measures that can be used
Basic rights	Medium	Medium	High	All
Obligations	Low	High	Low	All
Implementation	High	Low	Medium	SYB, SAS
Unique rights	High	Low	NA	EB, SYB, SAS

Notes:
NA - not applicable vis-à-vis the conceptual model of human rights
EB - events-based measures
SYB - survey-based measures
STB - standards-based measures
SAS - socio-economic and administrative statistics

to adopt in human rights measurement depends on the goals of measurement and the resources available for the purpose. A researcher would be expected to prioritize from the three components of measurement complexity, validity and viability and select an alternative best suited to his or her needs.

Summary

This chapter has sought to highlight the content of human rights as derived from international human rights law, with the purpose of establishing clarity in its monitoring and measurement. The first section described the international system of human rights protection, also known as the international human rights regime, as well as its regional counterparts. The subsequent section mapped the distinct contours of the concept of human rights. We suggested that this concept could be understood at three levels: the basic level related to the core content of human rights; the secondary level, which highlighted the constitutive elements of the concept; and the indicator/data level, which operationalized these elements into distinct measures. The final section of this chapter presented a comparative account of the trade-off between complexity, validity and viability of the measurement of this concept. Researchers and social scientists continue to grapple with making human rights easier to measure, understand and interpret. The next chapter presents the rationale behind human rights measurement and the usefulness of social science methods in this endeavour.

3 Measuring human rights

The previous chapter argued that human rights are moral claims that have been accorded legal recognition and that states are legally obliged to ensure that they respect, protect and fulfil these claims. The chapter sidestepped the thorny issue of the absence of agreed philosophical foundations for human rights and concentrated on what state and non-state actors have articulated about rights through the development of the international human rights law. In this way, the chapter argued that the *content* of human rights has been developed through the proliferation *of* international law and through the deliberations *within* international legal fora and the associated mechanisms and institutions for the enforcement of human rights. The empirical referents for measuring and monitoring human rights, however, are how these rights are protected in *principle*, realized in *practice* and promoted through *policy* (Landman 2004, 2006). The framework we develop as a result thus establishes and delineates the many categories, dimensions and principles of human rights that are in need of measurement, and further outlines different approaches to 'operationalizing' the content within the framework for the development of the measures themselves (i.e. basic rights, obligations, implementation and unique rights).

Despite the development of a framework for the content, dimensions and principles associated with human rights that ought to be measured, *how* is the concept of human rights converted into a measure and in what ways have human rights been measured to date? This chapter provides answers to these two questions. First, it adopts a model of measurement from Adcock and Collier (2001) to show how social scientific measurement moves through four different levels ranging from general background concepts (i.e. human rights), through systematized concepts (i.e. the core content of human rights) and their operationalization, to scores on human rights across units of analysis (e.g. a high score on civil rights $CR \uparrow$ in country X in year T). Second, it provides a general overview of existing measures of human rights, including events-based measures, standards-based measures, survey-based measures, and socio-economic and administrative statistics. Each of these examples has in some degree undergone the process of operationalization outlined here, while the discussion reveals *how* and *why* that process is vulnerable to problems of bias and error that could affect the validity, reliability and meaning of the measures themselves. The chapter, thus, paves the way for the ensuing four chapters, which present a much fuller discussion of each of these methods of measurement.

The moment of measurement

What are the operational steps that allow analysts to move from the different conceptual distinctions of human rights to the provision of valid, meaningful and reliable measures? At an abstract methodological level, the process of measurement converts well-defined and well-specified concepts into meaningful quantitative measures or qualitative categories, and has four main levels (Adcock and Collier 2001, also Zeller and Carmines 1980). For Adcock and Collier (2001), the first level concerns the *background concept* that is to be measured, which is the broad constellation of meanings and understandings associated with the concept. The content outlined in the previous chapter summarizes what comprises such a broad constellation of meanings and understandings in the field of human rights. The second level develops the *systematized concept*, which specifies further the concept that is to be measured, such as a specific right (e.g. the right not to be tortured) or a group of rights (e.g. civil rights). Here, the many different categories and lists of human rights enumerated in the various international human rights instruments and their different dimensions as outlined in the previous chapter provide a good starting point for our understanding of such a systematized concept. The third level *operationalizes the systematized concept* into meaningful, valid and reliable indicators, such as events-based, standards-based, survey-based, or other measures (see the next section of this chapter). It is at this level that either new indicators are developed and constructed for the systematized understanding of human rights or existing data are used as suitable indicators and/or proxy measures. The final level provides *scores on indicators* for the units of analysis being used, whether these are individuals, groups, countries, regions, etc. Figure 3.1 depicts these four levels graphically.

Consider a concrete example. The *background concept* to be measured is human rights, the scope and content of which has been *systematically* developed in the ways that were outlined in Chapter 2 and comprise Levels 1 and 2 depicted in Figure 3.1. For example, the right not to be tortured is a systematized concept of human rights that has been identified most notably in the *Universal Declaration of Human Rights* (UDHR), the *International Covenant on Civil and Political Rights* (ICCPR), and the *Convention against Torture* (CAT). The systematized concept is susceptible to operationalization at Level 3. Given the different dimensions of human rights outlined in our framework, the right not to be tortured can be measured at this level *in principle* (i.e. does the state have a legal framework in place to prevent torture and has the state ratified the relevant international instruments that prohibit torture); *in practice* using events-based data, standards-based data and/or survey-based data, which measure the degree to which torture is practised within the jurisdiction of the state

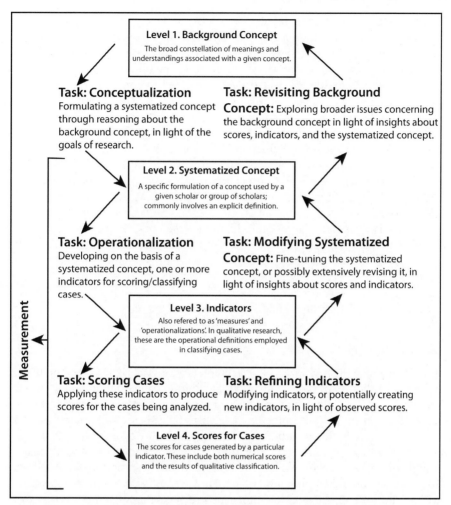

Figure 3.1 Conceptualization and measurement: levels and tasks
Source: Robert Adcock and David Collier, "Measurement Validity: A Shared Standard for Qualitative and Quantitative Research", American Political Science Review, Volume 95(03): pp 529-546, (2001)

and by whom; and in *policy* terms, such as the resources a state is investing in procedures, policies, reforms and training for the prevention of torture throughout the justice sector.

Level 4 measurement refers to the actual scores on units for this right. For example, the main unit might be Brazil in the year 1985, also known as a country-year data point in large-scale cross-national data sets. The different scores on this unit might be Brazil's ratification status of the ICCPR and CAT (a measure of principle); the number of acts of torture committed in that year (an events-based measure); the relative severity and frequency in the use of torture in that year on a scale from 1 to 5 (a standard-based measure); the average public perception of the severity and frequency of torture (a survey-based measure); and the proportion of governmental expenditure as a percentage of annual Gross Domestic Product (GDP) dedicated to combating torture, and the number of police in receipt of human rights training as a means of sensitization and education, cases of reprimand for torture, etc. (a set of policy measures). This example shows that any one systematized concept of a human right can have several different indicators that measure different aspects of that right, which may or may not be showing the same general pattern. It is well known that a country's ratification status says nothing about its actual human rights practices (see, e.g. Keith 1999; Hathaway 2002; Hafner-Burton and Tsutsui 2005, 2007; Landman 2005a; Neumayer 2005). Beyond the descriptive analysis of patterns across the different indicators, second-order analysis of some of them might examine the degree to which certain groups experience more torture than other groups, such as the urban poor and/or landless peasants in the rural sector, which would constitute a measure of discrimination (see, e.g. Amnesty International 2007; Human Rights Watch 2007; US State Department 2007; Landman and Larizza 2009).

Source material

Moving through the four levels of measurement, however, is predicated upon the existence of thorough, up-to-date and reliable source material on human rights practices of states, within states and, in some cases such as migration and minorities, between states. Certainly, the increase in the salience of human rights as an issue of international importance combined with organizations dedicated to documenting human rights violations means that there is now a greater availability of comprehensive information on actual practices of states and the conditions under which individuals live. However, this information necessarily will be 'lumpy', biased and incomplete, since reporting of human rights violations is fraught with difficulties, including fear from victims, power of the offenders, comprehensive evidence and quality of communications technology, among others. In recognizing this problem, Bollen (1992: 198) argues that there are six levels of information on human rights violations: (1) an *ideal* level with *all* characteristics of *all* violations (either reported or unreported), followed by (2) recorded violations, (3) known and accessible violations, (4) locally reported violations (nation-state), (5) internationally reported violations, and (6) the most biased coverage of violations, which may include only those reported in the USA. The early behaviourist attempts to measure political violence used only the *New York Times Index* for its source of information (e.g. Taylor and Hudson 1972; Taylor and Jodice 1983). Now, the catchphrase on the masthead for the *New York Times* is 'all the news that's fit to print', which clearly shows that its coverage is inherently biased. The index covered a lot of countries for cross-national analysis, but the coverage on each country was very thin.

In another example, a comparative project on social movements in Europe used the Monday edition of two national newspapers in each of the comparator countries on the assumption that Europeans are more likely to protest at the weekend (see Koopmans 1996). While the move to multiple newspapers is a good one, the bias in only using Monday papers undermines the measurement and analysis of protest events. The lessons from these examples are equally applicable to human rights projects. Indeed, Ball's (2000) analysis of violence in Guatemala showed that newspaper coverage was inversely related to detailed accounts from other sources (see also Hoover et al. 2009). Newer approaches on dissent and repression use multiple newswire sources that are machine coded to alleviate some of the problems of relying on single sources (Francisco 2000, 2004a, 2004b), but newspaper coverage itself is a function of the market for reporting and the decisions of the editorial staff. Other work seeks to obtain lower levels of information in much greater detail. For example, the *Torture Reporting Handbook* (Giffard 2000) and *Reporting Killings as Human Rights Violations* (Thompson and Giffard 2002) are manuals that define specific rights, outline the legal protections against their violation, and provide ways in which testimony and evidence from victims can be collected, although there are very few examples of projects that have then gone on to collect such data systematically. The Human Rights Information and Documentation System (HURIDOCS) provides standards for human rights violations reporting and now represents a vast network of human rights groups (Dueck 1992: 127).

While such increased information at all levels is helpful for systematic human rights research, there remains a trade-off or tension between micro levels of information gathering and the ability to make systematic comparative inferences about human rights. The trade-off is between the *intensiveness* (i.e. detailed and in-depth coverage of smaller units of analysis) and the *extensiveness* (i.e. more generalized coverage of a larger number of units of analysis) of information. In the former case, such as the data collection and analysis carried out by truth commissions, strong inferences about the dynamics of human rights violations can be analysed thoroughly, but these inferences are limited to the single country from which the data were collected. In the latter case, less intensive data collection and the use of equivalent measures to 'travel' for comparative analysis means that more general inferences can be drawn, but that there will necessarily be some loss of information (see also Landman 2000, 2003 and 2008).

As the ensuing four chapters show, efforts in the development of human rights measures of all types have begun to pay more attention to the link between the type, number, and quality of sources of information that are then used to convert abstract concepts of human rights into reliable measures. The debates over source material and bias have generated their own literature within the field of human rights methodology, and have been a feature of articles and debates in the social sciences more generally. The key insight from these debates is to recognize the presence of bias and the potential for error, and then put in place a series of steps to minimize the error. Such a set of concerns affects all the types of measures outlined in this chapter and in the rest of this volume.

Types of human rights measures

The move through the four levels of measurement from background concepts to scores on units, regardless of the sources of information, shows that there are many different ways in which to measure human rights. There remain significant trade-offs in the types of data available that measure human rights directly and the types of analysis that are made possible with them. First, as Chapter 4 shows, there are very good but limited collections of highly disaggregated forms of human rights events data available for a handful of countries that have experienced prolonged authoritarianism, foreign occupation, or civil war (see Jabine and Claude 1992; Ball et al. 2000; Ball et al. 2003; Landman 2006a; Silva and Ball 2007). These data are on gross violations and are coded using multiple sources of information, such as statements collected by official truth commissions, monitoring systems developed by non-governmental organizations (NGOs), analysis of morgue records (e.g. Haiti) and cemeteries (e.g. East Timor), or some form of retrospective survey instrument (e.g. East Timor) (see Landman 2006a: 107–25; Silva and Ball 2007).

Second, as Chapter 5 shows, there are more extensive (but less intensive) collections of human rights data for many countries (150 < N < 194) over time (25 years < T < 36 years) that are of a more general nature and capture broad trends in the protection of certain human rights (see Jabine and Claude 1992; Landman 2002, 2006a). These data are coded from a variety of sources (some of which are not explicitly reported) in which some form of a standardized scale is derived from a deep reading of narrative accounts on general trends in different categories of human rights, and have, by-and-large, relied on the annual reports produced by either the US Department of State or Amnesty International (see below). Third, as Chapter 6 shows, there are survey-based measures that capture attitudes, perceptions, and experiences of human rights (good and bad) that rely on random samples, some form of cluster sampling, or targeted sampling of 'at risk' groups in particular political contexts. Finally, as Chapter 7 shows, there are socio-economic and administrative statistics that capture different structures, processes, and outcomes within countries that have a bearing on human rights.

Like other trade-offs in the social and policy sciences, scholars are faced with similar sets of trade-offs engaging in research using these different forms of data, while recognizing the different types of inferences made possible through the analysis of different samples of countries. To date, the published social scientific literature engages in either the statistical analysis of pooled cross-national time-series (PCTS) data sets or small-N comparative and single case studies that make little use of available events data (although for a notable exception, see Brockett 2005; see also Landman 2005a, 2005b, 2006a). Nevertheless, efforts to develop systems for human rights measurement

have advanced both within the discipline of political science and among other
human rights scholars and practitioners, covering more categories and
dimensions of human rights using a variety of measurement strategies. It is to
these different types of human rights measures that the discussion now
turns.

Events-based measures

Events-based data answer the important questions of what happened, when it
happened and who was involved, and then report descriptive and numerical
summaries of these events. Counting such events and violations involves
identifying the various acts of commission and omission that constitute or
lead to human rights violations, such as extra-judicial killings, arbitrary
arrest, or torture. Such data tend to be disaggregated to the level of the violation itself, which may have related data units such as the perpetrator, the
victim and the witness, as well as the place where and date when the violation
took place (Ball et al. 2000; Landman 2006a: 82–83). As Chapter 4 shows,
events-based data analysis has a long tradition dating back to a 1930s analysis of data on 15,000 'quasi-judicial' executions carried out during the height
of the Reign of Terror after the French Revolution. Since then, events-based
data have featured in the political science literature on social revolution,
social protest and social movements, labour mobilization and strike activity,
civil war violence and events linked to international conflict (Gurr 1969, 1970;
Tarrow 1989; Tilly 1993; Tilly et al. 1975; Foweraker and Landman 1997;
Francisco 2000, 2004a, 2004b). Similar analyses on human rights violations
have been carried out for the more contemporary cases of Guatemala (Ball
2000), Peru (Ball et al. 2000), Kosovo (Ball and Asher 2002), East Timor
(Silva and Ball 2007) and Colombia (Guzmán et al. 2007). In each of these
studies, highly disaggregated forms of violations data are used to estimate the
total number of violations that have occurred (usually extra-judicial killings
and disappearances), the temporal and spatial patterns in the data, and any
ethno-political dimensions that might demonstrate that particular groups
suffered disproportionately. In his comparison of El Salvador and Guatemala,
for example, Brockett (2005) uses time-series events-based data on social protest
and patterns of state repression to show how state violence in Guatemala
virtually eliminated a popular rural movement while in El Salvador similar
levels of state violence did not.

Standards-based measures

Standards-based measures of human rights are one level removed from event
counting and violation reporting, and merely apply an ordinal scale to qualitative information. The resulting scale is derived from determining if the reported
human rights situation reaches a particular threshold of conditions, ranging
from good (i.e. few violations) to bad (i.e. many violations). The most dominant

examples of standards-based measures include the Freedom House scales of civil and political liberties (Gastil 1978, 1980, 1988, 1990; www.freedomhouse. org), the 'political terror scale' (Mitchell et al. 1986; Poe and Tate 1994; Gibney and Stohl 1996), a scale of torture (Hathaway 2002), and a series of seventeen different rights measures collected by Cingranelli and Richards (www.humanrightsdata.com). Across these scales, different checklists are used to judge the degree to which rights are protected and are used to convert a qualitative account (or accounts) into a standard scale that provides a comparable measure of human rights across a large selection of countries. For example, Freedom House provides measures for almost all the countries in the world from 1972, while the political terror scale covers over 150 countries since 1976, and the Cingranelli and Richards data are for over 160 countries since 1980.

While these scales have been primarily developed to measure the *de facto* realization of human rights (or what we call 'rights in practice'), other scholars have used the standards-based idea to code the *de jure* commitment of states to the promotion and protection of human rights (what we call 'rights in principle'). In this kind of application, the standard scale denotes the degree to which a state signs, ratifies and files reservations to the various international human rights treaties that have been passed since the 1948 UDHR. In these coding schemes, countries are rewarded for treaty ratification and punished for the degree to which their reservations undermine the object and purpose of the treaty. Keith (1999), Hathaway (2002), Neumayer (2005), and Hafner-Burton and TsuTsui (2005, 2007) use simple dummy variables for ratification, while Landman (2005b) includes state signature alongside ratification and then combines the ratification variable with a weighting variable for the filing of state reservations.

Survey-based measures

Survey-based measures of human rights move away from the reliance on narrative accounts of violations or conditions and collect data on human rights using structured or semi-structured survey instruments applied to a sample of individuals. Typically, the sample is large and random such that inferences can be drawn about the target population. Long the workhorse of the social sciences and market research, survey data have been less used in social scientific research on human rights than either events-based or standards-based measures. They have usually featured more often in research on the support for democracy (e.g. Kaase and Newton 1995), trust and social capital (e.g. Whiteley 1999, 2000), patterns of corruption (www.transparency.com), or as components of larger indices of 'post-material' values (see Inglehart 1997). Increasingly, though, household surveys have been used to provide measures for popular attitudes about rights and to uncover direct and indirect experiences of human rights violations. Some of the most notable work has been carried out by the NGO Physicians for Human Rights, which conducts surveys of 'at risk' populations (e.g. internally displaced people or women in conflict) to determine the nature and degree of human rights violations. The 'minorities at risk' project certainly captures the degree to which communal groups and other national minorities suffer different forms of discrimination (see www.cidcm.umd.edu/mar). In another example, the truth commission in East Timor carried out a retrospective household mortality survey on all births, deaths and illnesses within the country during the period of Indonesian occupation between 1974 and 1999. The survey data were then matched with other kinds of data collected from statements given to the truth commission and from a census of all graveyards. These multiple sources of data were then used to estimate the total number of people who had died during the occupation using a log-linear method of estimation common in biological and epidemiological research (see International Working Group for Disease Monitoring and Forecasting 1995; Ball et al. 2003; Silva and Ball 2007).

Survey analysis and public opinion research has also begun to explore the degree to which citizen attitudes and perceptions about human rights are in line with the actual human rights situation in countries. This research combines the standards-based indicators of human rights outlined above with random sample surveys that ask questions about respect for human rights, where typical response categories include such terms as 'a lot', 'some respect', 'not much respect', and 'no respect at all' (see Anderson et al. 2005; Richards 2006). The research then compares the perceptions of the human rights situation to the general trends in the protection of different categories of human rights either for the world (Richards 2006), or broken down for particular regions (Anderson et al. 2005; Richards 2006). The global comparisons reveal that citizens have multiple rights referents when they formulate assessments on the human rights situation in their own countries, and that there is a moderate congruence between public opinion about the human rights situation and the actual human rights situation, which is further differentiated across regions (Richards 2006: 28–31). Across the post-communist states of Central and Eastern Europe, there is a high congruence between perceptions of human rights and actual human rights practices, but this congruence tends to be stronger for more highly educated citizens (Anderson et al. 2005). Both studies represent the application of cross-cultural analysis using perceptions of human rights as a main subjective variable of interest as it relates to more objective human rights conditions, even though standard-based measures themselves have a large degree of subjectivity.

Socio-economic and administrative statistics

Socio-economic and administrative statistics produced by national statistical offices or recognized international governmental organizations have been increasingly seen as useful sources of data for the *indirect* measure of human rights, or as indicators for *rights-based approaches* to different sectors, such as justice, health, education, and welfare (see UNDP 2006). As Chapter 7 shows, government statistical agencies and intergovernmental organizations produce a variety of socio-economic statistics that can be used to approximate measures of human rights. For example, academic and policy research has used aggregate measures of development as proxy measures for the progressive realization of social and economic rights. Such aggregate measures include the Physical Quality of Life Index (PQLI) and the Human Development Index (HDI). In both cases, the indices have been used to track both the *level* of development and the *change* in development, both of which are then linked to the notion of *fulfilling* social and economic rights (see Chapter 2). For some, the PQLI represents a measure of subsistence rights (Milner et al. 1999), since it captures the fundamental aspects of an individual's life and those basic requirements for human existence. For others, the PQLI can be compared to other measures in ways that capture a state's achievement in the area of economic and social rights (see Cingranelli and Richards 2007). The measure is derived from the combination of a socio-economic statistic and a standard-based measure that captures the idea of 'government effort to respect economic rights' (ibid.: 224).

In any such application, however, these measures are imperfect since they provide little information on the degree to which different groups in society enjoy the benefits of development. They are aggregate measures of macro-economic performance and, in the absence of a breakdown by gender, ethnicity, religion and other social categories traditionally associated with exclusion, such measures do not yet capture rights dimensions. Other measures, such as the percentage of women or minority groups in society that achieve levels of literacy and/or education, and the breakdown of households with access to available housing, health and other social welfare services can serve as indicators for the presence of possible discrimination against certain groups in the exercise of their social and economic rights. It is typical for national statistical offices to collect on an annual basis a variety of socio-economic indicators that, in principle, should be disaggregated by gender, age, income and geography in ways that can provide proxy indicators for economic and social rights; however, owing to capacity issues and limited resources, sample sizes make it difficult to disaggregate these kinds of data.

Measuring to assess

The measurement of human rights is not something that is only relegated to academic studies and analysis, but increasingly, as we note in the Introduction to this volume, has become of interest to international donor agencies, intergovernmental organizations and governments themselves, particularly the Organisation for Economic Co-operation and Development (OECD) countries, which have an obligation to extend a proportion of their annual GDP to developing countries. Indeed, the 'Make Poverty History' movement carries with it the expectation that countries will contribute at least 0.07 percent of their GDP to overseas development assistance. However, the extension of aid without accountability from the recipient has become a thing of the past, as donors seek to examine the state of governance within recipient states (or partner countries as they are also known) as a condition of that aid and assistance. One crucial aspect of the attention towards governance is the promotion and protection of human rights within the partner country. Thus, donors need valid, reliable and meaningful indicators on human rights and some kind of integrated framework of assessment with which to analyse the indicators.

While the development of such frameworks is ongoing and highly variable across the OECD countries, donors have generally taken two approaches to the use of governance assessments and their links to the extension of foreign assistance. In the first approach, assessment is directly linked to the idea of a country 'score card', and threshold conditions are set that determine the degree to which a partner country will continue to receive assistance. Both the World Bank with its Country Policy and Institutional Assessment (CPIA) framework, and the USA with its Millennium Challenge Account (MCA) establish a direct link between a country's achievement of governance above a certain threshold and the extension of aid. Of the 16 criteria that comprise the CPIA, there are four with direct links to human rights, including gender equality; social protection and labour; property rights and rule-based governance; and transparency, accountability and corruption in the public sector (see World Bank 2007). Of the 17 criteria used by the MCA, there are six with direct links to human rights, including civil liberties; political rights; voice and accountability; rule of law; control of corruption; and land rights and access (see www.mcc.gov/selection/indicators/index.php). Such an approach is meant to encourage improvement across the elements of the framework with a view to improving governance and, as a consequence, tackling poverty and ensuring more equitable economic development.

In the second approach, assessment is seen as a way to determine areas of need, which are then linked to different aid modalities such as government budget support, sector-wide funding and particular project funding in discrete areas of need. Both the United Nations Development Programme (UNDP) and the UK Department for International Development (DFID) have adopted this kind of approach, and both organizations have fully integrated human rights into their use of governance assessment. With the publication of its 2006 *White Paper Making Governance Work for the Poor*, DFID recognized the inexorable link between good governance and development in general and to poverty reduction in particular. Its definition of good governance includes explicit reference to the protection of human rights as found in the UDHR, as well as the various international treaties for the promotion and protection of human rights. It committed itself to carrying out governance assessments on all partner countries and to include human rights within these assessments. The policy shift was partly due to a recognition that human rights are part of the development agenda and partly due to the fact that the 1998 Human Rights Act obliges all UK government agencies to mainstream human rights into their work.

Across the UNDP and DFID (among other donor agencies) there has been the recognition that the use of and over-reliance on externally derived human rights and other governance indicators have become increasingly untenable for practical and normative reasons. Practically, donors need to work with partner governments and elements of civil society and an over-reliance on external subjective scales (e.g. the standards-based scales outlined in this present volume) can cause problems on the ground, since local stakeholders afford them little credence and such scales rarely shed light on the sub-national reasons for variation in human rights. Normatively, the use of such scales undermines the key human rights principles of participation and inclusion that lie behind rights-based approaches to development as laid out in the UN Common Understanding on a Human Rights-Based Approach to Development. There has, thus, been a call within UNDP and DFID to generate indicators that are locally owned and suitable for sub-national time-series analysis (see UNDP 2004: 4–20).

These various precedents set within the international donor community suggest that human rights measurement will continue to feature as a key component of overseas aid policies and that more work is needed in establishing indicators that meet the various requirements of disaggregation, time-series, local ownership, etc. There is, to date, no agreed framework of assessment, since donor needs, priorities and policy orientations are different, as are the geographical areas in which their work is concentrated. For this volume, however, we offer a preliminary set of assessment steps that draw on the International Institute for Democracy and Electoral Assistance's (International IDEA) democracy assessment framework (see Beetham et al. 2008), which is committed to the principle that it is only the citizens of a country who have the ability and authority to assess the quality of their democracy, governance and/or human rights. This general principle does not exclude the use of foreign experts or externally derived indicators, but it does insist on nationally-based research teams providing the core content of any assessment. Beyond this general commitment, though, it is important to stress that human rights assessments have many purposes, different mixtures of content and priorities, different uses of indicators and benchmarks, as well as methods for engaging with a larger audience, whether that is the donor community in general, a specific donor agency, or other countries within the region and beyond. Accordingly, the set of steps that we summarize in Figure 3.2 relate to carrying out a human rights assessment, where there is a direct link between the initial purpose of an assessment through the use of human rights measures of the kind outlined in this volume (i.e. the range of sources used), to the ways in which an assessment 'markets' itself and disseminates its results.

Summary and the way forward

This brief overview of available measures of human rights shows that there have been concerted efforts to convert abstract philosophical and legal

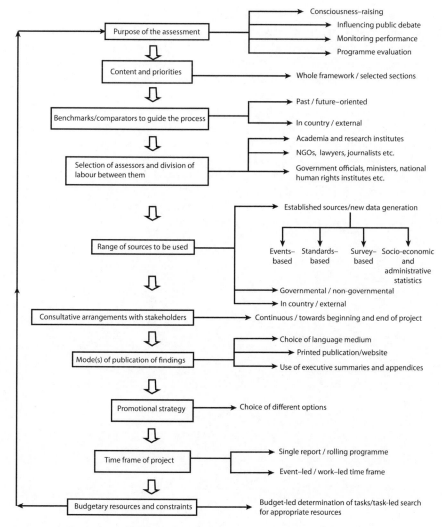

Figure 3.2 Preliminary decisions for a human rights assessment
Source: adapted from Beetham et al. 2008: 43

concepts into valid, reliable, and meaningful measures for use in systematic social scientific analysis. These efforts have not only sought to develop measures that are more closely related to the different categories and dimensions of human rights, but also address the methodological challenges associated with source materials on human rights. As we shall see in the ensuing chapters, the efforts to develop measures have primarily focused on the variable government respect for civil and political rights. Less effort has been dedicated to providing measures of the protection and fulfilment of civil and political rights and even less effort has been dedicated to providing measures of economic and social rights. The paucity of data on these different dimensions and categories of rights beyond civil and political rights is partly explained by the ideological and philosophical underpinnings of American political science, which has been behind the development of many of these measures, and by the methodological difficulty of finding quantitative expression for economic and social rights. The next four chapters do show, however, that despite these various lacunae in the measurement of human rights, considerable progress has been made to meet the demand for better measures. The chapters chart that progress from events-based data through to socio-economic and administrative statistics and discuss the assumptions, challenges and limitations associated with each kind of data, while recognizing all the time that human rights are an elusive and in many ways unobservable social phenomena, which are not always tractable for measurement.

4 Events-based measures of human rights

Introduction

One dominant aspect of social phenomena susceptible to social scientific analysis includes what have broadly been described as 'events'. Events in the social world include large occurrences, or 'macro' events, such as elections, military coups, transitions to democracy, social revolutions, international and civil wars, foreign interventions and invasions, social protests and labour strikes, government crackdowns (i.e. the 1989 Tiananmen Square massacre or the Myanmar (Burma) military response to the 2007 'Saffron' revolution), and significant market crashes (e.g. the 1929 market crash, the 1982 'debt crisis', or the 1997 Asian financial crisis). They also include small or 'micro' events, such as village skirmishes and raids, personal and organized crimes, public lynching, looting, sexual violence, bribery and other corrupt acts, denial of access to services, consumer and commercial firm choices, among countless others. There is a long tradition in the social sciences in the analysis of such events that has included qualitative comparative history of macro events (e.g. Wolf 1969; Womack 1969; Skocpol 1979; Wickham-Crowley 1993) and quantitative comparative analysis of macro events (e.g. Small and Singer 1983; Cioffi-Revilla 1990, 1991, 1996; Cioffi-Revilla and Lai 1995; Cioffi-Revilla and Landman 1999). The behavioural revolution in the social sciences led to the development of increasingly sophisticated ways to capture, measure and analyse macro and micro events using quantitative analysis. Such data have been collected on cross-national samples of countries that extend across the entire globe and stretch far back into history, including patterns of war in ancient China (Cioffi-Revilla and Lai 1995) and the rise and fall of Mayan city states (Cioffi-Revilla and Landman 1999; also Diamond 2005). Outside the academic world, events-based data have become increasingly important in significant strategic and foreign policy debates on warfare and conflict, such as the debate surrounding the number of civilian deaths as a result of the 2003 invasion of Iraq (see Burnham et al. 2006; www.iraqbodycount.org; Johnson et al. 2008) and the estimations and analysis of political violence in Colombia, in particular during the process of demobilization (Ball et al. 2008; Giles 2008).

This chapter shows how the tradition of events-based data analysis has been applied to measuring human rights. It argues that human rights events are highly complex and comprise a number of discrete features that are susceptible to coding, aggregating and analysing in ways that help explain and understand patterns and variation in human rights violations across time and space. Using events-based measures can approximate the duty to *respect* human rights as well as the duty to *protect* them. In this sense, the state is only one of many agents that can violate human rights, where history shows that many other agents can be responsible for violating human rights, such as guerrilla movements, insurgency organizations, death squads, criminal organizations and so-called 'uncivil movements' (Payne 2000) to name a few. Many of the efforts to measure human rights examined throughout this volume have focused on the state as the main agent of violation, while the developments in the field of events-based data analysis can fully incorporate non-state actors. Indeed, the events-based data analysis conducted on the case of armed conflict in Peru between 1980 and 2000 showed that *Sendero Luminoso*, or 'Shining Path', a non-state (and anti-state) Maoist revolutionary movement was found to have been the perpetrator that carried out the largest proportion of killings and disappearances (see Ball et al. 2003).

This chapter first outlines the main methodological dimensions of events data in general and for human rights in particular, including the nature of an event, the appropriate units of analysis and the complexity of a human rights event. It then turns its attention to problems associated with source material for human rights events data, including the non-random nature of event reporting and the use of multiple sources and 'multiple systems estimation' (MSE). It then examines the application of events-based data in the human rights field, including their use in truth commissions and other human rights data projects, and concludes with a general assessment of events-based data as one form of human rights measurement.

Events data in the social sciences

One of the first applications of statistics to the study of violence analysed the patterns in more than 15,000 'quasi-judicial' executions carried out during the height of the Reign of Terror (March 1793 to August 1794) after the French Revolution. Using the archived documents of the tribunals that sentenced people to death, Greer (1935) analysed the patterns of sentencing and executions over time, space, and by social class (nobles, upper-middle class, lower-middle class, clergy, working class, and peasants). His analysis of time-series patterns in executions by social class and across different *départements*, showed that the peasants and working classes suffered the largest number of executions, where the majority of the executions (52 percent) took place in the west, followed by the south-east (19 percent) and Paris (16 percent). In this analysis, the *individual victim* (or suspect) served as the *basic unit of analysis*, while the 'event' was the act of sentencing and/or execution carried out by the regime against the individual. Using the individual as the basic unit of analysis allowed for secondary analysis and further testing of empirical propositions about the causes of the sentencing and executions, such as those based on class, political, economic and/or religious variables (Greer 1935: 4). The inferences drawn from the analysis of the patterns, however, only extended to the known cases that formed the official archives of the Reign of Terror, where it is very likely that many acts of execution occurred that were simply not recorded (a significant point that forms part of the methodological discussion below).

In line with Greer's (1935) study of violence in France, the 'behavioural revolution' in the social sciences moved analysis away from large social processes and structures to key features, characteristics and outcomes of human behaviour. The initial impulse within the movement was to disaggregate the study of human behaviour down to the individual level of analysis in an effort to build general theories and models that would be universally applicable across human societies. Accompanying this shift in analytical focus were efforts to construct large and complex data sets comprising multiple variables, which measured a wide range of features relating to the human condition, where events data featured heavily. For example, from the early work of Seymour Martin Lipset (1959) onwards, the political development literature (see Cammack 1997 for a comprehensive review) is replete with analyses that use large cross-sectional data sets comprising indicators on all aspects of social, economic, and political development. In a similar fashion Gurr's (1969; 1970) seminal work on political violence used events-based variables such as 'deaths from political violence' collected from a large sample of countries around the world, while separate projects were solely dedicated to collecting, collating, and providing machine-readable data sets for subsequent analysis (e.g. Jodice and Taylor 1976; 1983; Banks 1994). Work on political violence among academics continues very much in this vein, where efforts are dedicated to providing more valid, reliable, and meaningful measures of political violence (see, e.g. Francisco 2000, 2004a, 2004b).

While this tradition of social scientific research initiated in many ways by Greer (1935) sets an important precedent for events-based approaches to human rights, more recent efforts led primarily from the human rights nongovernmental sector have made great advancement in the coding and analysis of events-based data that has direct applicability to human rights. This work had been led by the Human Rights Data Analysis Group founded at the American Association for the Advancement of Science (AAAS) in Washington, DC, which moved to Benetech, a social justice technology organization based in Palo Alto, California in 2003. The advancements have included greater attention to the source material used for coding human rights violations, using the violation and not the individual person as the primary unit of analysis, and the application of statistical techniques most appropriate for estimating 'unknown' populations of events from a known but non-random selection of source material. Before examining this important work, however, it is first necessary to outline the main methodological issues associated with events-based data and how these need to be addressed for the development of events-based measures of human rights.

The methodology of events data

Analysing events in the field of human rights involves overcoming a number of challenges related to the nature of the event, the unit of analysis, the complexity of the event itself, the type of source material available, and the ability to overcome inherent biases in the source material. At a basic level, events share a number of characteristic features. They have a start date (also known as an *onset*) and an end date, where the difference between the two is understood as the event *duration*. They have various dimensions of *magnitude* and *size*, including the number of actors involved (e.g. individuals, groups, regions, countries, organizations, etc.), the types of things that actors do, and the types of things that happen to them (e.g. violence, liberation, suppression). For example, the American Civil War began on 10 April 1961, had a duration of four years, was estimated to have had 650,000 fatalities, and comprised two main belligerents: the Union and the Confederacy (see Cioffi-Revilla 1998: 46). Human rights events have similar sets of features, which can be broken down into their constituent parts and counted in ways that provide meaningful measures of violations.

Work on political violence tends to focus on individual deaths, where often the perpetrator, context and other defining features of the death remain obscure. For human rights analysis, it is precisely this obscure information that needs to be uncovered in ways that provide deeper explanation and understanding of what happened and why it happened in a particular context. The unit of analysis can be the event itself, individual people involved in the event, or the violations committed during the event. It is to this latter unit of analysis that the most recent advances in events-based data analysis have turned, since the structure of a human rights event is highly complex. The metaphor used is one of the 'grammar' of the human rights event, where it is essential to break down the perpetrator (and his or her associated features), the victim (and his or her associated features), the act (or acts) committed, and the defining features of the event, such as the time, context, etc. Like Lasswell's (1951) notion of politics being about 'who gets what when and how', the Human Rights Data Analysis Group at AAAS developed the 'who did what to whom' model of a human rights event (see Ball et al. 2000). The particular breakthrough in developing their model was to focus on the violation as the basic unit of analysis and how that unit links all the other elements of a human rights event together.

Figure 4.1 captures the complexity of a human rights event that is typically found in a statement taken by a human rights non-governmental organization or an official truth commission. The figure shows that any single statement contains information about victims, violations, and perpetrators. One or many victims have definitive characteristics, may have suffered one or many different violations, committed by one or many perpetrators. There is, thus, a series of complex interrelationships between and among violations, victims and perpetrators. From this information, different dimensions of the human rights event can be extracted. For example, individuals have different *identities* (peasant, worker, man, woman, indigenous, rich, poor) and *roles* (perpetrators and victims), which can be contained in a statement that is collected. Victims and perpetrators can be individuals, groups and organizations. Violations can include a whole range of human rights abuses, which emerge *inductively* from the testimonies that are provided and *deductively* through application of a 'controlled' vocabulary to the set of violation acts that are reported in the testimony. Like perpetrators, victims can be individuals, groups, institutions and organizations. In addition, there are important temporal and spatial dimensions to a human rights event that can be analysed using this model.

While an initial list of violations may emerge *inductively* from the testimonies, the use of controlled vocabularies reduces the complexity of the information *deductively* to a certain degree by providing the core content of violations that are to be analysed, boundary conditions to distinguish between violations, and counting rules to provide continuity over time and across space. The general dimensions of such a vocabulary and set of boundary conditions are agreed upon by the non-governmental organization (NGO) collecting the information or the truth commission in advance, while leaving some room for adjustment as the information from statements begins to be processed. The core content of violations can come from international human rights law, human rights violation documentation organizations (e.g. HURIDOCS), or can emerge as a consensus among leaders and analysts within the organization collecting the information.

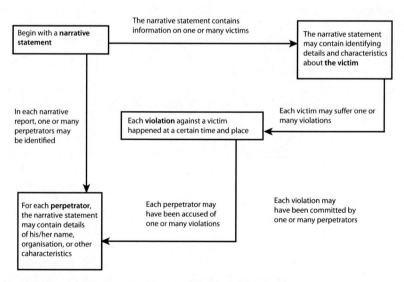

Figure 4.1 The complexity of a human rights event
Source: adapted from Ball, Spirer and Spirer 2000b: 29 and published previously in Landman 2006: 112

Whatever the case, the organization responsible for coding the data needs to provide full public disclosure of its method to ensure accountability of the process to users of the data, as well as reliability to those wishing to replicate the data.

This model for collecting and analysing human rights events data remains a relatively flexible instrument, which can be used by different organizations investigating human rights abuses that have taken place under very different circumstances. Examples of applications of this model in the field include seven truth commissions (El Salvador, Haiti, South Africa, Guatemala, Peru, Sierra Leone, and East Timor), the 'book of the dead' project in Bosnia (Ball et al. 2007), the analysis of extra-judicial killings in Chad (Human Rights Watch 2005), the analysis of migration and killings in Kosovo (Ball and Asher 2002), counting and reporting 'cross-fire killings' by the Rapid Action Batallions in Bangladesh (Human Rights Watch 2006), and ongoing efforts at estimating political killings in Colombia (see Guzmán et al. 2007; and also Ballesteros et al. 2007).

The model's focus on *violations* as the unit of analysis means that crucial information that is often lost by only counting deaths (or other units) can now be counted and analysed. For example, it is typical within human rights events that a victim will suffer multiple violations (e.g. detention, torture and then killing). Counting only the death (or extra-judicial killing) will over-represent the killings and under-represent other types of violations, leading to a miscounting that could bias the analysis and assessment of a human rights situation in a country. In similar fashion, any focus on 'the most egregious' violations (a typical legal boundary condition of truth commissions) will necessarily undercount other types of violations that may have occurred. For example, under a system that records only the most egregious violations, victims that had been detained, tortured and then killed would only have their death registered, while the other violations would go unreported. If this occurs then any time-series analysis of patterns in human rights violations may make incorrect assessments of trends in particular types of violations.

For example, in the Recovery of Historical Memory Project (REMHI) in Guatemala the category of 'massacre' was used to code events that were too messy to disentangle. The initial results of the analysis under-reported the number of human rights violations, which had been obscured by lumping together many different violations that occurred during a massacre. Many people in the massacres had been raped, tortured and disappeared, but were not coded as having suffered those violations. Thus, when the massacre and non-massacre data were combined, there was an under-representation of the true nature of the human rights violations that had occurred (Mazariegos 2000: 156). A similar problem occurred as part of the work carried out by the United Nations Mission for the Verification of Human Rights in Guatemala (MINUGUA). It initially coded 'primary' violations suffered by victims (i.e. those that were most serious) and, therefore, grossly under-represented the 'victimization' of the individual and created a 'false view of the events and distortion of trends' (Ward 2000: 138). Using the violation as the basic unit of analysis can, thus, alleviate some of these problems of misrepresentation of the true nature and pattern of human rights violations.

Source material

Events-based human rights data rely on three particular types of source material: (1) 'found' data, (2) narrative data and (3) official statements. Found data include such data as archival records (as in the case of data analysed in Chad), border data on refugees (e.g. in Kosovo), morgue records (e.g. in Haiti), exhumations (as in the case of Kosovo) and even gravestones, which often contain names, dates, and cause of death (e.g. in East Timor). Narrative accounts are those stories of human rights abuse and human rights events reported to non-governmental agencies, human rights activists and newspaper reporters. Official statements are those narrative accounts formally collected through the use of statement forms by truth commissions, in which individual deponents are given the opportunity to provide a detailed account of single or multiple human rights events. In each case, the raw source material is then given quantitative expression through event coding, which then allows for descriptive and second order statistical analysis to identify patterns, trends and tendencies in the data from which larger inferences about the human rights situation can be drawn. There is, thus, an attempt to analyse in systematic fashion the human rights events that have been reported or recorded initially in narrative fashion.

By definition, found data literally come in the form in which they are found, and will yield significant information to the degree that they were properly organized in the first place. For example, in the case of its analysis of prison records found in Chad, Human Rights Watch and the Human Rights Data Analysis group at Benetech had relatively complete records and were able to match surnames and remove duplicate entries to provide preliminary conclusions about the victims of the Habré government. In similar fashion, the border records obtained by Ball and Asher (2002) contained detailed information about the movement of people within Kosovo, including their village of origin, dates of departure, first name, and surname. In both cases, the written records were converted into database files and analysed for patterns using variants of the 'who did what to whom' model. In the case of the Kosovo analysis, Ball and Asher (2002) used descriptive statistics to show how the movement of refugees matched the trends observed in data on killings coded from exhumations, while their secondary analysis showed that the majority of activities from the Kosovo Liberation Army (KLA) and NATO bombings were not related to the patterns in migration or killing; a finding that was used against Slobodan Milosevic in hearings conducted by the International Criminal Tribunal for the Former Yugoslavia (ICTY).

In contrast to found data, there is more of an opportunity for narrative statements to be collected systematically. Casual and 'off the record' conversations with reporters are not particularly systematic and decisions to include particular reports in published news media are a function of editorial decisions that respond to market conditions and the political climate within particular countries. However, human rights organizations and truth commissions dedicated to collecting narrative statements can put systems in place that record and archive information in ways that make quantitative coding possible. Experience in the field has shown that key pieces of information such as the name, date of birth and other vital data can be recorded in standardized ways, while the statement itself is best if it is recorded in an open-ended fashion, after which coding teams can apply a controlled vocabulary to the statement. For example, the South African Truth Commission experimented with different kinds of statement forms and found that using abridged forms led to significant losses in data that proved unsatisfactory (see O'Sullivan 2000; Wilson 2001). The Peruvian Truth and Reconciliation Commission drew on the experiences in South Africa and other truth commissions to develop a much more 'open' form, on which deponent statements were recorded. Politically and psychologically, such an approach provides the deponent a sense of importance and dignity, freedom and openness, and inclusion and participation in the process. Methodologically, the approach can yield significantly more data on human rights violations and the context under which they were committed than more restricted approaches, since the deponent is permitted to provide a free-flowing account of an event that is then coded after the statement has been taken. Such an approach stands in stark contrast to survey-based human rights data, in which respondents are often restricted in the answers that they may give by the questions that they are asked.

All three types of source material in events-based data are typically 'non-random' in nature, which is to say, individual victims, witnesses and/or relatives of victims come forward *voluntarily* and offer their particular story about a human rights event, which is then coded into quantitative information. The use of a non-random sample means that the information being used for coding human rights events-based data is biased. There are any number of reasons why an individual will or will not come forward to bear witness to a human rights event, and the non-random nature of the source material means that human rights events could be over-reported in some instances and under-reported in other instances, making it difficult to draw secure inferences about the general state of human rights abuse within a particular context from the sample of information that is provided. It is typical in statistical studies to make inferences from a sample to a population. In survey analysis, for example, a random sample of respondents is used such that general statements about the entire population of interest can be made, and that when they are made, they are accompanied by an associated 'margin of error', which is a function of the sample size itself. The presence of non-random samples means that the inferences can only be made to the sample itself.

The truth commissions in El Salvador, Haiti, South Africa, and Sierra Leone all used single, non-random samples, which meant that any summary statistics used in their final reports make reference only to those events reported and do not make inferences to the entire population of violations that may have been committed. The final reports thus contain general language such as 'there were N instances of human rights abuse (e.g. unlawful detention, torture, extra-judicial killing) reported to the truth commission'. In this way, truth commissions and other human rights documentation projects that only use single, non-random samples will necessarily be limited in the types of inferences that they can make about a particular context. For example, the Bosnian 'book of the dead' project comprises 246,736 cases of victims, of which there are multiple records for 96,985 victims, and a detailed assessment of the database cautions that it still contains particular sets of biases, for example, with respect to the reporting (or misreporting) of victims by civilian or military status (see Ball et al. 2007). There are, thus, significant limitations to events-based data that have been collected and coded using only one non-random sample of deponents, even if such projects have used the 'who did what to whom model'.

Failure to address the non-random nature of the source material can lead to significant problems and controversy in the human rights community. For example, in the case of Colombia, a debate has developed surrounding an assessment of the efficacy of paramilitary demilitarization in reducing the trends in extra-judicial killing. On one side of the debate are a series of scholars and NGO members who have used police data to show that patterns in lethal violence have declined and that paramilitary demobilization is the main cause for that decline (Spagat and CERAC 2006; Gonzalez Peña and Restrepo 2006). On the other side of the debate are the data analysts at Benetech who claim that both the descriptive statement about the decline in lethal violence and its cause are fallacious and unsubstantiated by the statistical evidence (Ball et al. 2008). At the crux of the debate is the use of a single source of human rights information – the Colombian National Police Registry of Homicides (DIJIN) – to make larger inferences about the decline in violence and its putative cause. Since it is only one source of information, the claim that violence has declined assumes that the Colombia police database has recorded all known instances of homicide. If this assumption can be challenged (and it can for the reasons outlined above) then any subsequent causal analysis that seeks to attribute the decline to a particular variable or set of variables is necessarily insecure. While this particular debate is far from settled, it raises an important set of issues that all human rights scholars and practitioners need to confront when seeking to use events-based data.

The key solution to overcoming the inherent biases in using single, non-random samples has been to employ what is called 'multiple-systems estimation' (MSE) in which multiple samples of information are used, compared and analysed for the degree to which particular victim information appears across different sources.[1] This statistical approach was pioneered in Denmark to estimate fish populations (Peterson 1896; Bishop et al. 1975)[2] and has since become a staple method in epidemiological studies (International Working Group for Disease Monitoring and Forecasting 1995a, 1995b; LaPorte et al. 1995; Chao and Tsay 1998; Zwane and van der Heijden 2005), urban policy studies (Bishop et al. 1975), and now human rights events data analysis (see Ball et al. 2000; Ball et al. 2003; Landman 2006a: 117–20). The simplest version of the technique uses two sources of information and the basic assumption is that the ratio of the number of people that have been 'captured' in both source 1

and source 2 to the number of people 'captured' in source 1 is proportional to
the ratio of the number of people captured in source 2 to the number of people
in the entire population. In formal terms, these ratios for a simple two-source
version of MSE appear as follows:

$$\frac{\text{Individuals in both Source 1 and Source 2}}{\text{Individuals in Source 1}} = \frac{\text{Individuals in Source 2}}{\text{Total number of people}}$$

This means that multiplying the number of sources increases the ability to
make a more accurate estimate of the total number of human rights violations
that have taken place (see Box 4.1). While this example uses only two sources,
it is possible to increase the number of sources, which produces better estimations with smaller margins of error. For example, the events-based data
analysis carried out by the truth commissions in Peru and East Timor used
three different sources, as did the *post hoc* analysis of killings in Guatemala.
MSE yields an estimate with an associated margin of error, much like the type
of statistics used in public opinion polling data. In the Peruvian case, the
truth commission estimated that 69,280 people had been either killed or had
disappeared, with a margin of error which had a lower limit of 61,007 and an
upper limit of 77,552. These estimates were made from three sources of data
that had information on 24,692 victims (see Ball et al. 2003; Landman 2006a:
121). By comparing, matching, and analysing the presence and absence of
these victims across the three samples, the analysis was able to estimate a total
number of killings and disappearances that far exceeded previous reports or
the expectations of the truth commission itself, and was able to show geographical and ethnic differentiation in the patterns of killing (Ball et al. 2003).
In the Guatemalan case, MSE not only provided an estimation of the total
number of people killed in the civil war (between 119,300 and 145,000), but
also showed that indigenous people were six times more likely to be victims of
the violence (Ball 2000b).

Box 4.1 Multiple systems estimation

There are many demands for statisticians to provide reasonable estimations
of unknown populations, such as the number of people who have been
immunized in a given area, the number of heroin addicts in a particular
urban area, the number of feral dogs in a city centre, or the number of fish
in a particular body of water. In all these examples, the total population
is *unknown* but *circumscribed*, which is to say there is an upper limit to
the number in the population, or a *boundary* that defines the maximum
number of the particular population that is to be estimated. Statisticians

have devised a way in which more accurate estimations of unknown populations can be calculated, by examining multiple sources of information about that same population. Devised in the late 19th century to estimate fish populations in Denmark, multiple systems estimation (or MSE) uses the different probabilities associated with any one individual appearing across different sources of data to estimate the total number of individuals in the population, plus or minus a margin of error.

In the field of human rights, MSE has solved the problem of estimating the number of particular kinds of human rights violations by examining different sources of information that have been collected in any given context. There are three possibilities of a relationship across different sources of information: (1) no overlap of sources, (2) partial and complex overlap of sources, and (3) complete overlap of sources (see Figure 4.2). The task of the analyst is to uncover the degree to which there is an overlap across sources, control for the bias in coverage rates of each of the sources (i.e. some may have large coverage and others small coverage, and all the sources may cover most of the violations or very few of the violations), and estimate the total population once the features of the sources are known. Interestingly, the larger the degree of overlap across the sources, the more accurate estimate can be made (i.e. the smaller the margin of error).

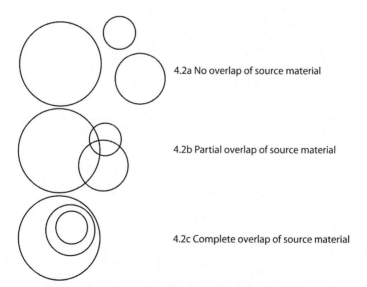

4.2a No overlap of source material

4.2b Partial overlap of source material

4.2c Complete overlap of source material

Figure 4.2a-c Multiple sources and the degree of overlap
Source: adapted from http://hrdag.org/resources/mult-systems-est.shtml

Consider a hypothetical example of two sources of information that have been collected on nine different individuals (see Figure 4.3). Source *A* has information on individuals 1 through 6, while source *B* has information on individuals 5 through 9. Both *A* and *B* have information on individuals 5 and 6. The combination of *unique* reporting and *overlap* in reporting is crucial for the ways in which MSE calculates the total number of individuals (usually those who have been killed). The overlap area is denoted M, while the total population to be estimated is denoted N. There are different probabilities associated with individuals being reported or 'captured' by the different sources. The probability that an individual is captured by source A is A/N, by B is B/N, and by both A and B is M/N. There is also a ratio between those individuals captured (A, B and M) to the total number of individuals in the population to be estimated (N). The ratio of the number of individuals captured in A and B (M) to the number of individuals captured in A is proportional to the ratio of the number of individuals captured in B to the total number of violations (N), such that M/A = B/N. Using algebraic reduction and transformation, MSE uses the following formula to estimate the total number of individuals in a population: N = AB/M (see Ball et al., 2003: 20).

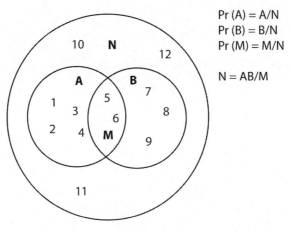

$$Pr\,(A) = A/N$$
$$Pr\,(B) = B/N$$
$$Pr\,(M) = M/N$$

$$N = AB/M$$

Figure 4.3 Multiple systems estimation (MSE) with two sources
Notes:
N= the total population to be estimated
A= First source with data on individuals 1–6
B = Second source with data on individuals 5–9
M = Overlap between A and B with data on individuals 5 and 6
Individuals 10–12 have not been captured by any source
Source: Adapted from Landman 2006: 118

The full estimation relies on a further set of assumptions whose potential violation can be managed through the use of additional sources of information and different specifications of statistical models that capture the degree of dependence between and among the different sources. MSE has been applied successfully in the analysis of human rights violations in Guatemala, Peru and East Timor.

The use of events data

Across these different data projects there has been significant learning and innovation, such that now the preferred method for generating events-based human rights data is to use the 'who did what to whom' model with multiple systems estimation. Table 4.1 summarizes a set of data projects to date that have used events-based data to measure human rights (and in particular extra-judicial killings), including the country, the type of project, the number of sources, the use of MSE and examples of some of the findings. The table shows that truth commissions feature heavily in their use of events-based data since in many ways their mandates and legal epistemology are very much based on the idea of victims of atrocities and thus demand an accounting of past periods of wrongdoing that increasingly have included more robust attempts at estimating the total number of people killed, the temporal and spatial patterns to those killings and, when possible, the key factors that explain the patterns that have been observed (see Landman 2006a: 107–25). The data collection and analysis methods that were developed through these experiences have travelled well to other projects, such as those in Chad and Kosovo, the results of which have led to the provision of an evidence base from which to advocate for redress and justice.

It is clear from the table that despite the development and learning within the truth commission sector, not all projects have used the 'who did what to whom' model and not all have been able to use MSE. For example, the CERAC data project in Colombia codes events according to the 'conflict event' itself rather than the 'violation' as in the 'who did what to whom' model, and then estimates the number of killings that have been reported to have resulted from the event using a cross-referencing system with archives and other sources such as human rights NGOs (see Restrepo et al. 2006: 102–3); however, the data are not assembled in the 'who did what to whom' format, nor are the final event count data produced using MSE. Those projects using the 'who did what to whom' model, such as those in Kosovo and Chad, use the individual killing or other violation as the basic unit of analysis. For the absence of MSE in some of the examples, many projects had begun collecting and coding data before the application of MSE to human rights had been developed. In addition, the nature of some country contexts and projects precluded the use of three sources, while in others, creative solutions were found to develop additional sources. In the case of East Timor, which had no history of human rights organizations collecting narrative accounts of human rights abuse during the period of Indonesian occupation, the data project combined data from the 8,000 statements with data from a graveyard census and retrospective household survey to create three different sources of information (Silva and Ball 2006).

The table shows that those projects that used MSE (e.g. Peru and East Timor) were able to make inferences about human rights violations (e.g. extrajudicial killings) that relate to the total population of violence and not just to those events that have been reported. Thus, in Peru, the final estimation of killings and disappearances ranges from a minimum of 61,007 to a maximum 77,552 dead, where the most likely estimate is 69,280 (Ball et al. 2003). In other words, MSE produced an estimation of 69,280 and margin of error of approximately ±7,000. In similar fashion, the estimation of total dead in East Timor ranges from a minimum of 90,000 to a maximum of 124,000, with the likely estimate to be 102,800 (i.e. a margin of error of ±12,000) (see Silva and Ball 2006). Moreover, the combination of MSE and the 'who did what to whom' model allowed for further inferences to be drawn. In Peru, the analysis was able to show that 46 percent of all deaths and disappearances were caused by the guerrilla movement *Sendero Luminoso*, with 30 percent caused by state agents and 24 percent by other actors in the conflict (Ball et al. 2003). In East Timor, the combination of MSE and the 'who did what to whom' model allowed the data analysts to estimate that between 17,600 and 19,600 deaths were as a direct result of intentional killing, and between 73,200 and 95,200 deaths were attributed to hunger and illness over and above natural pre-invasion rates (Silva and Ball 2006). In both examples, since the deaths themselves were the main units of analysis, the use of MSE and the 'who did what to whom' model could link *particular perpetrators* or causes to *particular victims* and then aggregate the data for general sets of inferences about the main dimensions of the human rights context under investigation. These types of estimates and inferences are not possible in the absence of MSE and the 'who did what to whom' events data model.

Assessing events data for measuring human rights

It is clear that tremendous progress has been made in the collection, coding, and analysis of events-based data with respect to measuring human rights. This form of data has many distinct advantages for providing valid, reliable and meaningful ways to measure and analyse large-scale human rights violations. The evolution of methods from early coding of 'deaths from political violence' to the 'who did what to whom model' and MSE has firmly established this mode of measurement in the field of human rights. In countless commentaries, popular perceptions, and much empirical and normative theorizing, human rights violations are often thought of in terms of what one

Table 4.1 Example of events-based human rights measurement

Type of project		Number and type of sources	Who did what to whom?	MSE[a]	Descriptive features	Examples of estimations of human rights violations
Truth Commissions						
	El Salvador (1992–1993)	Truth commission 2 NGOs	Yes	No	7,000 by truth commission; 22,000 in total with 3,000 duplicated	60% of statements concern extra–judicial killings, 35% forced disappearance, 20% torture
	Haiti (1995–1996)	Truth commission Morgue survey	Yes	No	7,000 by truth commission	8,667 victims suffered 18,629 violations
	South Africa (1995–1998)	Truth commission Human rights documentation project	Yes	No	21,296 by truth commission	46,696 reported violations 36,935 reported gross violations 28,750 reported victims
	Guatemala (1997–1999)	Truth commission 2 NGOs	Yes	Yes	7,517 by truth commission 5,465 by REMHI[b] 5,000 by CIIDH[c]	Between 119,300 and 145,000 dead, with the most likely estimate being 132,000; REMHI reports 52,427 victims
	Peru (2001–2003)	Truth commission 5 NGOs	Yes	Yes	16,917 by truth commission	23,969 reported dead 18,397 fully identified dead 61,007 to 77,552 dead with most likely estimate being 69,280

(continued on next page)

Table 4.1 (continued)

Type of project	Number and type of sources	Who did what to whom?	MSE[a]	Descriptive features	Examples of estimations of human rights violations
Sierra Leone (2000–2005)	Truth commission	Yes	No	7,000 by truth commission	40,242 total violations reported 7,983 forced displacements reported 5,968 abductions reported 4,835 arbitrary abductions reported 4,514 killings reported
East Timor (2001–2005)	Truth commission Household survey Graveyard records	Yes	Yes	8,000 by truth commission 1,396 households 250,000 graveyard records	90,000 to 124,000 total dead with the likely estimate to be 102,800. Between 17,600 and 19,600 deaths were as a direct result of intentional killing, while between 73,200 and 95,200 deaths were attributed to hunger and illness over and above natural pre–invasion rates.
Other					
Bosnia Book of the Dead	Mixed data sources but all collated into one database	Yes	No	246,736 records, but many incomplete	At least 96,895 people have been confirmed as dead, but this number is seen as the minimum and not the full total

(continued on next page)

Table 4.1 (continued)

Type of project	Number and type of sources	Who did what to whom?	MSE[a]	Descriptive features	Examples of estimations of human rights violations
Lethal violence in Colombia, 1988–2002	Police data base of homicides	No	No	CERAC data set on conflict events	CERAC counts 32,280 total deaths for the entire period
Chad	Prison records	Yes	No	A set of written documents found in a prison storeroom containing multiple records and references to individuals that were detained.	12,321 different victims recorded in 'found' documentation
Kosovo	Border records Exhumations	Yes	Yes	Combination of different sources of data allow for time–series and inferences about possible causes of trends.	52,043 refugees forced to migrate 1,316 people killed

[a] Multiple systems estimation; [b] Recovery of Historical Memory Project, Guatemala; [c] International Centre for Investigating Human Rights, Guatemala.

Source: Kritz 1995; Ball, Kobrak and Spirer (1999); Ball, Spirer and Spirer (2000); Hayner (2002); Ball, Asher, Sulmont and Manrique (2003); Final Report of the South African Truth and Reconciliation Commission (1998); Final Report for the Truth and Reconciliation Commission for Peru (2003); Final Report of the Truth and Reconciliation Commission for Sierra Leone (2004); Restrepo, Spagat and Vargas (2006: 109); Spagat, M. and CERAC (2006); Ball and Asher 2002; Ball, Tabeau, Verwimp 2007.
Updated and adapted from Landman 2006: 111

socio-political actor does to another and under what conditions (e.g. see Wantchekon and Healy 1999; Ignatieff 2001; Mitchell 2004; Landman 2006a: 37–45). Thus, the notion of the 'grammar' of a human rights event, however complex it might be, has an intuitive appeal and using the violation as the basic unit of analysis coupled with MSE allows for sophisticated statistical analysis, which provides the kind of scientific evidence that holds up under quite strict conditions and which can be used in testimony against major perpetrators of crimes against humanity (Ball and Asher 2002).

Moreover, the 'who did what to whom' model has proved flexible enough to 'travel' to a variety of different political contexts around the world, ranging from developing countries such as South Africa to poor countries such as Liberia, Sierra Leone and East Timor. Interestingly, the social scientists and statisticians involved in the Bosnian 'book of the dead' project established their version of the model *independently* from and in ignorance of the original development of the model by the Human Rights Data Analysis Group at the AAAS. The model, thus, has an intuitive appeal that can be grasped across the globe and applied in a variety of very different human rights situations. Once the data are collected and coded, the standard descriptive and analytical techniques from statistics can be applied to provide robust portraits of trends, patterns and, in some cases, causes of large-scale human rights violations; inferences that refer to the previously 'unknown' population of violations and not just to the set of violations that have been reported to an official body or human rights organization.

Thus far, the application of the 'who did what to whom' model and MSE has been restricted to a limited set of civil and political rights that have been violated under time-bound and extreme conditions. In theory, however, it is entirely possible for these two methods to be applied to economic and social rights and to be used as the basis for a system for monitoring everyday forms of human rights abuse (i.e. those that occur as a function of statecraft and not during periods of conflict, authoritarian rule and foreign occupation). As we outlined in Chapter 2, the dimension to respect and protect across both main sets of human rights refers to intentional acts by state and non-state actors, which may or may not lead to a violation of rights. Thus, the 'violations' approach upon which the 'who did what to whom' model is based can be used to count such events as the denial of medical treatment to ethnic minorities, discrimination in education, mistreatment of workers, and a multitude of other violations of economic and social rights in which a *plausible countable unit* can be identified. If this argument is extended further, it is possible to use these techniques to measure economic crimes, acts of corruption and other practices that have relevance to human rights standards and principles.

Despite the many advantages of these kinds of data for measuring human rights, there are a number of limitations. First, any kind of events coding, and the 'who did what to whom' model in particular, is extremely time consuming. It requires the development of the controlled vocabulary upon which the research and data team agrees; multiple coding teams and inter-coder reliability tests (see Chapter 5 on standards-based measures); and sufficient hardware and knowledge of computer programming to manage and manipulate large and complex data files. Second, to date the available events data on human rights have been collected for periods of authoritarian rule, violent conflict and foreign occupation and not on everyday forms of human rights abuse collected on an annual basis as part of a process of monitoring and documentation. The collection of data has often been governed by context-specific factors, which make cross-national and time-series comparisons of the kind demanded by academics and policy makers difficult. Third, as noted above, the development and application of methods for coding these data have thus far focused on the respect and protection of civil and political rights and not economic and social rights (see also Chapman 1996). This does preclude events-based data coding for economic and social rights, but no such project has been developed.

Summary

This chapter has shown that events-based data are very much part of the social sciences and have been developed in ways that provide a suitable method for measuring human rights. From the early days of the behavioural revolution to the current application of the 'who did what to whom' model and MSE, events-based data have been used to map the trends, patterns and contours in the violation of particular sets of human rights. The 'grammar' of a human rights event can be deconstructed, coded, aggregated and then analysed to provide valid, meaningful and reliable measures of human rights for academic, advocacy and policy purposes. Events-based data have been particularly useful for official truth commissions and data projects that seek to document particular moments of history in which large-scale violations of human rights have taken place. Future developments in the events-based data ought to include moving beyond moments of crisis to become a way in which everyday violations can be monitored, and moving beyond counting deaths and disappearances to other violations of human rights.

5 Standards-based measures

Introduction

We saw in the last chapter that events-based measures of human rights grew out of a larger tradition in the social sciences on political violence and political events, such as strikes, demonstrations and other political manifestations. These measures were then developed in particular ways that have become useful in monitoring, documenting and analysing large-scale human rights violations. Standards-based measures have a similar history in that they, too, have developed out of a larger tradition in the social sciences that sought comparability in measures and indicators for cross-national and time-series statistical analysis. This effort at providing comparable measures for cross-national research has included developing measures for democracy (e.g. the Polity measures), warfare (e.g. Correlates of War), corruption (International Country Risk Group), and governance (e.g. World Bank) (see Landman and Häusermann 2003). Moreover, since the emergence of the 'good governance' agenda, there has been a demand from intergovernmental and governmental donor agencies and policy makers for such measures to use in the allocation of international aid and other decisions. Both the Millennium Challenge Account in the USA and the World Bank use standards-based measures for passing judgement on the performance of governments and allocate foreign aid accordingly. Standards-based measures of human rights have developed in parallel to these other efforts and in certain instances have been included as measures of these other concepts, or as components of measures that combine different kinds of indicators into country level indices (e.g. the World Bank governance measures).

The label 'standards-based' comes from the fact that they code country-level information about human rights on a standardized scale that typically is both ordinal and limited in range. This means that the scale values denote 'better' and 'worse' protection of human rights, while the range of the values themselves is limited to a few values per scale. For example, as we shall see below, the Freedom House Civil and Political Liberties scales range from 1 (good protection) to 7 (bad protection); the Political Terror scale ranges from 1 (good protection) to 5 (bad protection); and many of the rights scales in the Cingranelli and Richards human rights data project range from 0 (bad protection) to 2 (good protection). The standardization of the scales assumes that each scale applies equally to all countries in the world and provides the ability for analysts to compare performance on certain sets of human rights across space and over time. In this way, there is a 'universality' assumption built into the scales, since the same set of criteria for coding are applied to every country.

This chapter provides an outline and assessment of these different standards-based measures of human rights. The first section examines the background to these measures, which in many ways began with political science efforts to code regime types using simple systems which typically divided the world between democracies and non-democracies, and various categories of regime in between the two (e.g. Lipset 1959; Fitzgibbon and Johnson 1967; Dahl 1971; Duff and McCamant 1976; and Jaggers and Gurr 1995). The next section examines the most popular efforts at developing standards-based measures for human rights, starting with Raymond D. Gastil's work on freedom (later to be taken over by Freedom House), the political terror scale developed at Purdue University and now housed at the University of North Carolina Asheville, Oona Hathaway's (2002) scale of torture, and Cingranelli and Richards' ongoing project of developing measures for different sets of human rights. The section also considers the attempts at providing measures for the *de jure* commitments states make by coding treaty ratifications (e.g. Keith 1999; Hafner-Burton 2005; Landman 2005) and reservations (Landman 2005a). The final section considers the main limitations to these kinds of measures, including the types of source materials that are used for the coding, the limited sets of human rights that have been coded using these methods, the validity and reliability of the coding process, aggregation bias, and the problem of 'variance truncation'.

Background: regime types and scales

In his seminal study on the relationship between economic development and democracy using cross-national quantitative data, Seymour Martin Lipset (1959) divided a sample of countries into four different groups that measured the relative degree of democracy or dictatorship. He divided European and English-speaking countries in his sample into stable democracies on the one hand and unstable democracies and dictatorships on the other. He divided the Latin American countries in the sample into democracies and unstable dictatorships on the one hand and stable dictatorships on the other. For the first group, those countries that had an 'uninterrupted continuation of political democracy since World War I, and the absence over the past twenty-five years of a major political movement opposed to the democratic "rules of the game"' were considered to be democracies (ibid.: 72, emphasis in original). The Latin American countries were classified as democratic if they 'had a history of more or less free elections for most of the post-World War I period' (ibid.: 72–73). The result of these divisions meant that Lipset had four groups of countries ranging across (1) stable democracies, (2) unstable democracies, (3) unstable dictatorships, and (4) stable dictatorships, which allowed him to compare different measures of economic performance. This division of countries into categories created what is known as a 'polychotomous' measure of democracy, while there is a further normative assumption behind the measure such that regime types range from more democratic to non-democratic.

The idea of providing categories that range in order from 'good' to 'worse' such as those found in Lipset (1959) established an important precedent for political science, and Lipset's work was soon followed by others who sought to develop measures of regime types, regime performance, or regime repressiveness. In following Lipset, Fitzgibbon and Johnson created an 'image index' for types of governance in Latin America, which was derived using a standardized scale and a survey of country experts who provided ratings for countries on a five-year basis between 1945 and 1985. The original questionnaire contained general social and political variables (e.g. education, income, well-being, free and competitive elections, free party organization, scrutiny of the executive, etc.) scored on a scale ranging from 1 to 5, which was then revised in 1975 to include only the political variables and the scale was changed to range from 1 (most democratic) to 20 (least democratic) (see Fitzgibbon and Johnson 1967; Johnson 1976, 1977, 1981; Wilkie and Ruddle 1992; see also Foweraker and Landman 1997: 56–58).

Other efforts to measure democracy followed these general ideas in devising coding schemes that reward countries for having more democratic practices (and fully developed democratic institutions), including Robert Dahl's measures for his concept of polyarchy (subsequently developed by Coppedge and Reinicke 1988, 1990, 1991), the 'Polity' project, which provides standards-based scales on components such as executive constraint and the competitiveness of the nomination process, which are aggregated into a single democracy score (Jaggers and Gurr 1995); Banks's (1994; 1997) institutional scales of democracy for 115 countries between 1850 and 1997 (see also Foweraker and Landman 1997, Appendix B, 251–52), and Bollen's (1998) global index of liberal democracy for 1950–90. In each of these examples, the use of standards-based scales provides a comparable set of measures that allow for descriptive mapping of trends in democracy and more sophisticated secondary analysis on increasingly large pooled cross-section time-series (PCTS) data sets.

The application of standardized scales to measuring human rights began with Duff and McCamant (1976), who devised a measure of repression that used four components coded on a four-point scale, yielding a final scale that ranges from 0 (no repression) to 16 (full repression). Their definition of repression is as follows:

> ... the use of government coercion to control or eliminate actual or potential political opposition. Coercion may come in the form of arrests and imprisonment or exile of individuals who oppose or are suspected of wanting to oppose the government. It may also come in the form of denial of due process to these individuals. The government may prevent opponents from associating and organizing. It may deny them the right to communicate through the media.

Such a definition fits squarely within the 'respect' dimension of civil and political rights as delineated in Chapter 2 on the content of human rights (see Figure 2.1). The coding for the scale included a four-point score being assigned across the following four components: (1) suspension of constitutional rights, (2) arrests, exile and execution, (3) political party restrictions and (4) censorship (see Table 5.1). Taken together, such a 17-point scale allows for a degree of within-country variation and between-country variation for descriptive and analytical comparisons that yield particular inferences about the general trends and explanations for the violations of particular sets of human rights.

Recent efforts: from 'freedom' to human rights

The more recent developments of standards-based measures of human rights have moved from fairly broad conceptions of the relative 'freedom' in a country (www.freedomhouse.org), to more narrowly defined sets of human rights that have in some cases included workers' rights, women's economic rights and women's social rights (see www.humanrightsdata.com), as well as measures of the *de jure* commitment of states to human rights through

Table 5.1 Duff and McCamant repression criteria

Component	0	1	2	3	4
Suspension of constitutional rights	No report of suspension	Temporary suspension (< 30 days)	Suspension > 30 days, but < 9 months	Suspension > 9 months, judicial interference	Complete suspension of legal procedures
Arrests, exiles, executions	None	small-scale (< 10 per million)	Large number of temporary arrests	Mass arrests (> 50); assassination	Large number of political prisoners or exiles, opposition leaders dead
Political party restrictions	No restrictions	Extremes excluded	All but small extremes allowed, some harassment of other groups	Control prevents a majority party	No opposition allowed
Censorship	No restrictions	Minor restrictions	Long term restrictions	Censorship of all political news, private ownership	Government directs what news is published

measuring the treaty ratification behaviour of states (Keith 1999; Landman 2005a). In each of these examples, the producers of the data have used source material on human rights practices within countries and applied coding protocols to the information to derive a set of standardized and comparable measures for cross-national and time-series analysis.

Freedom House

The first and most popular time-series standards-based measures of human rights were created by Raymond D. Gastil, which measures political rights and civil liberties on a scale of 1 (full protection and enjoyment of rights) to 7 (no protection or enjoyment of liberties). Gastil was primarily interested in the rights of individuals as they vary across countries. Freedom House, a non-governmental human rights organization primarily based in the USA sponsored the development of the scales and, in 1989, took over the job of coding countries using the original Gastil scale (Ryan 1994). In its disaggregated form, it provides a guide to the relationship between political and civil liberties over time. In its aggregated form, it shows the broad patterns in regime behaviour over time and in many ways measures the 'respect' dimension of civil and political rights (see Chapter 2). There were many criticisms of the Gastil scale (Barsh 1993), most of which focused on the ways in which the scores are coded from the source material. Gastil (1990) argued that he used a 'mental checklist' that roughly scored political liberties such as competitive elections, and civil liberties such as freedom of the press and freedom of expression. However, these general criteria have changed over the years and when Freedom House took over the coding, it published a complete checklist for both political and civil liberties (Ryan 1994), which are roughly the same as those employed by Gastil (see Tables 5.2 and 5.3).

These checklists were last updated in 2006 and the scoring system is now based on a checklist of 10 political rights questions and 15 civil liberties questions. The political rights questions are grouped into the three subcategories: electoral process (3 questions), political pluralism and participation (4), and functioning of government (3). The civil liberties questions are grouped into four subcategories: freedom of expression and belief (4 questions), associational and organizational rights (3), rule of law (4), and personal autonomy and individual rights (4). Points are awarded to these questions on a scale from 0 (small degree of rights and liberties present) to 4 (high degree of rights and liberties present). The resulting raw points scores thus have a maximum value of 40 for political liberties (i.e. up to 4 points for the 10 questions) and 60 for civil liberties (i.e. up to 4 points for the 15 questions). There is an additional discretionary question with respect to political liberties that may result in between 1 and 4 points being subtracted from the total score. These raw points scores are then converted into the two 7-point scales (see Table 5.4). The scales are comparable and rank countries from good protection and/ or enjoyment of rights and liberties (1) to bad protection and/or enjoyment of

Table 5.2 Freedom House checklist for political rights

Category	Main questions*
Electoral Process	Is the head of government or other chief national authority elected through free and fair elections? Are the national legislative representatives elected through free and fair elections? Are the electoral laws and framework fair?
Political pluralism and participation	Do the people have the right to organize in different political parties or other competitive political groupings of their choice, and is the system open to the rise and fall of these competing parties or groupings? Is there a significant opposition vote and a realistic possibility for the opposition to increase its support or gain power through elections? Are the people's political choices free from domination by the military, foreign powers, totalitarian parties, religious hierarchies, economic oligarchies, or any other powerful group? Do cultural, ethnic, religious, or other minority groups have full political rights and electoral opportunities?
Functioning of Government	Do the freely elected head of government and national legislative representatives determine the policies of the government? Is the government free from pervasive corruption? Is the government accountable to the electorate between elections, and does it operate with openness and transparency?
Additional discretionary questions	For traditional monarchies that have no parties or electoral process, does the system provide for genuine, meaningful consultation with the people, encourage public discussion of policy choices, and allow the right to petition the ruler? Is the government or occupying power deliberately changing the ethnic composition of a country or territory so as to destroy a culture or tip the political balance in favour of another group?

Note:
* There are numerous subsidiary questions to these main questions under each category.
Source: Adapted from the methodology section of the Freedom in the World web resource available at www.freedomhouse.org

these rights and liberties (7), which correspond to general conditions of rights and liberties in the countries (see Table 5.5).

Over the years, the Freedom House scales have been used as a measure of state repressiveness (Muller and Seligson 1987), the level of democracy (e.g. Burkhart and Lewis-Beck 1994; Helliwell 1994; Munck and Verkuilen 2002), the rule of law (Knack 2002), and now feature as one of the many components in the World Bank's measures of good governance (Kaufman et al. 1999a, 1999b, 2000, 2002). Despite this variety of uses for the scales, it seems that at a base level, they are measures of civil and political rights protection, and are best utilized in their separate form since combining them into a single index can produce biases. For example, a country with a score of 2 in its political

Table 5.3 Freedom House checklist for civil liberties

Category	Main questions
Freedom of expression and belief	Are there free and independent media and other forms of cultural expression? Are religious institutions and communities free to practice their faith and express themselves in public and private? Is there academic freedom and is the educational system free of extensive political indoctrination? Is there open and free private discussion?
Associational and organizational rights	Is there freedom of assembly, demonstration, and open public discussion? Is there freedom for non-governmental organizations? Are there free trade unions and peasant organizations or equivalents, and is there effective collective bargaining? Are there free professional and other private organizations?
Rule of law	Is there an independent judiciary? Does the rule of law prevail in civil and criminal matters? Are police under direct civilian control? Is there protection from political terror, unjustified imprisonment, exile, or torture, whether by groups that support or oppose the system? Is there freedom from war and insurgencies? Do laws, policies, and practices guarantee equal treatment of various segments of the population?
Personal autonomy and individual rights	Does the state control travel or choice of residence, employment, or institution of higher education? Do citizens have the right to own property and establish private businesses? Is private business activity unduly influenced by government officials, the security forces, political parties/organizations, or organized crime? Are there personal social freedoms, including gender equality, choice of marriage partners, and size of family? Is there equality of opportunity and the absence of economic exploitation?

Note: Adapted from the methodology section of the Freedom in the World web resource available at www.freedomhouse.org

Table 5.4 Converting Freedom House raw scores into the final 7 point scales

Political rights (PR) total Raw points	PR Rating	Civil liberties (CL) total Raw points	CL rating
36–40	1	53–60	1
30–35	2	44–52	2
24–29	3	34–43	3
18–23	4	26–33	4
12–17	5	17–25	5
6–11	6	8–16	6
0–5	7	0–7	7

Note: Adapted from the methodology section of the Freedom in the World web resource available at www.freedomhouse.org

Table 5.5 The Freedom House scales for political rights and civil liberties

Political rights	Civil liberties
Rating of 1 – Countries and territories that receive a rating of 1 for political rights come closest to ensuring the freedoms embodied in the checklist questions, beginning with free and fair elections. Those who are elected rule, there are competitive parties or other political groupings, and the opposition plays an important role and has actual power. Minority groups have reasonable self-government or can participate in the government through informal consensus.	**Rating of 1** – Countries and territories that receive a rating of 1 come closest to ensuring the freedoms expressed in the civil liberties checklist, including freedom of expression, assembly, association, education, and religion. They are distinguished by an established and generally equitable system of rule of law. Countries and territories with this rating enjoy free economic activity and tend to strive for equality of opportunity.
Rating of 2 – Countries and territories rated 2 in political rights are less free than those rated 1. Such factors as political corruption, violence, political discrimination against minorities, and foreign or military influence on politics may be present and weaken the quality of freedom.	**Rating of 2** – States and territories with a rating of 2 have deficiencies in a few aspects of civil liberties, but are still relatively free.
Ratings of 3, 4, 5 – The same conditions that undermine freedom in countries and territories with a rating of 2 may also weaken political rights in those with a rating of 3, 4, or 5. Other damaging elements can include civil war, heavy military involvement in politics, lingering royal power, unfair elections, and one-party dominance. However, states and territories with a rating of 3, 4, or 5 still enjoy some elements of political rights, including the freedom to organize quasi-political groups, reasonably free referendums, or other significant means of popular influence on government.	**Ratings of 3, 4, 5** – Countries and territories that have received a rating of 3, 4, or 5 range from those that are in at least partial compliance with virtually all checklist standards to those with a combination of high or medium scores for some questions and low or very low scores on other questions. The level of oppression increases at each successive rating level, including in the areas of censorship, political terror, and the prevention of free association. There are also many cases in which groups opposed to the state engage in political terror that undermines other freedoms. Therefore, a poor rating for a country is not necessarily a comment on the intentions of the government, but may reflect real restrictions on liberty caused by non-governmental actors.

(continued on next page)

Table 5.5 (continued)

Political rights	Civil liberties
Rating of 6 – Countries and territories with political rights rated 6 have systems ruled by military juntas, one-party dictatorships, religious hierarchies, or autocrats. These regimes may allow only a minimal manifestation of political rights, such as some degree of representation or autonomy for minorities. A few states are traditional monarchies that mitigate their relative lack of political rights through the use of consultation with their subjects, tolerance of political discussion, and acceptance of public petitions.	Rating of 6 – People in countries and territories with a rating of 6 experience severely restricted rights of expression and association, and there are almost always political prisoners and other manifestations of political terror. These countries may be characterized by a few partial rights, such as some religious and social freedoms, some highly restricted private business activity, and relatively free private discussion.
Rating of 7 – For countries and territories with a rating of 7, political rights are absent or virtually nonexistent as a result of the extremely oppressive nature of the regime or severe oppression in combination with civil war. States and territories in this group may also be marked by extreme violence or warlord rule that dominates political power in the absence of an authoritative, functioning central government.	Rating of 7 – States and territories with a rating of 7 have virtually no freedom. An overwhelming and justified fear of repression characterizes these societies.

Notes:
Countries and territories generally have ratings in political rights and civil liberties that are within two ratings numbers of each other. Without a well-developed civil society, it is difficult, if not impossible, to have an atmosphere supportive of political rights. Consequently, there is no country in the survey with a rating of 6 or 7 for civil liberties and, at the same time, a rating of 1 or 2 for political rights.
Source: Adapted from the methodology section of the Freedom in the World web resource available at www.freedomhouse.org

rights and 4 in its civil liberties is indistinguishable from a country with a score of 4 in its political rights and 2 in its civil liberties, if the analysis adds the two scores to equal 6. The data do provide comprehensive coverage of countries and time since 1972 and thus have been used throughout academic studies in economics, political science and international relations. For example, it is a simple matter to plot the trends in the scales over time for all the countries in the data set (see Figure 5.1), one country in the data set (see Figure 5.2), or to compare the relative protection of political rights and civil liberties across different regions in the world (see Figure 5.3). The data can also be subjected to more sophisticated statistical techniques, including correlation and regression analysis, which is why it remains popular within the academic and policy analysis communities. A fuller assessment of its limitations is provided in the next section of this chapter.

Political terror scale and the scale of torture

The dominant and, in many ways, more reliable standards-based scale of human rights is the 'political terror scale', which also was devised initially by Raymond Gastil in 1979. It was then taken up by Michael Stohl in 1983 and has since been updated by a variety of academics (Stohl et al. 1984; Stohl and Carleton 1985; Dixon and Moon 1986; Stohl et al. 1986; Gibney and Stohl 1988; Henderson 1991, 1993; Poe 1991, 1992; Gibney et al. 1992; Moon and

Figure 5.1 Mean Freedom House scores for political rights and civil liberties, 1976–2000

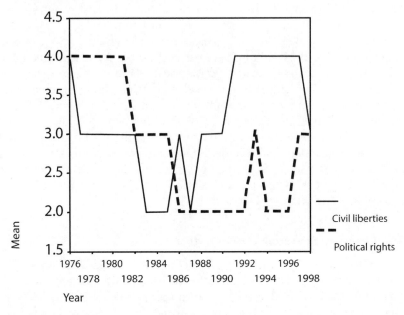

Figure 5.2 Mean Freedom House scores for political rights and civil liberties in Brazil, 1976–2000

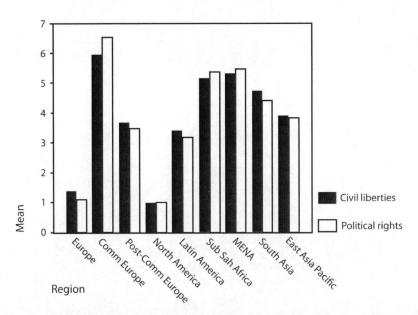

Figure 5.3 Mean Freedom House scores for political rights and civil liberties by region, 1976–2000

Dixon 1992; Poe and Sirirangsi 1993, 1994; Davenport 1995, 1996; Fein 1995). The political terror scale codes country performance (i.e. primarily human rights performance of the state) on a 1 to 5 scale using the annual reports produced by Amnesty International and the US Department of State. Others have labelled it as a measure of the protection of 'personal integrity rights', since it focuses on the state use of extra-judicial killings, torture, political imprisonment and exile (see Poe and Tate 1994; Poe et al. 1999; Zanger 2000). The five different levels of the scale code country human rights practices according to the different degrees and frequency with which political integrity rights violations are reported across both sources of information (see Table 5.6). The US Department of State typically reports on many more countries than Amnesty International, but the scale is produced for both sources, and social science analyses that have been conducted using the political terror scale treat them separately, although more recently, factor analysis has been used to find a common dimension among different standard-based scales of human rights (see Landman and Larizza 2009).

The political terror scale was originally coded by one team, but now uses multiple teams, which enhances its reliability (see Chapter 3). The procedure involves two different teams of coders, who code the country reports separately in the first instance and then compare their scores and resolve any differences. This method of multiple coding teams is similar to the method employed by truth commissions that adopted the 'who did what to whom' model for events-based data (see Chapter 4). In approximately 80 percent of the cases coded by the teams working on the political terror scale, coders have come up

Table 5.6 Political terror scale levels

Level	Description
5	Terror has expanded to the whole population. The leaders of these societies place no limits on the means or thoroughness with which they pursue personal or ideological goals.
4	Civil and political rights violations have expanded to large numbers of the population. Murders, disappearances, and torture are a common part of life. In spite of its generality, on this level terror affects those who interest themselves in politics or ideas.
3	There is extensive political imprisonment, or a recent history of such imprisonment. Execution or other political murders and brutality may be common. Unlimited detention, with or without a trial, for political views is accepted.
2	There is a limited amount of imprisonment for non-violent political activity. However, few persons are affected, torture and beatings are exceptional. Political murder is rare.
1	Countries under a secure rule of law, people are not imprisoned for their view, and torture is rare or exceptional. Political murders are extremely rare.

Source: www.politicalterrorscale.org/about.html

with the same score for the country in any given year, while discrepancies between the coders are adjudicated through the use of additional coders and the main academics in charge of the project. The coders are instructed to ignore their own biases, prejudices and perceptions of the countries and to limit their coding decisions to the information that is actually contained within the country reports provided by the Department of State or Amnesty International. Every attempt is made by the coders to remain conservative in the exercise of their judgement in ways that give countries 'the benefit of the doubt' and yield scores that are slightly more favourable than the report may suggest. Finally, coders use the additional insights provided by particular adjectives and other descriptors in making their judgements. For example 'reports of torture' is considered less extreme than 'widespread use of', which in turn is less severe than 'systematic patterns in', etc. (see www.politicalterrorscale.org).

The methodological strengths of the political terror scale have led to its adaptation by Hathaway (2002: 1970–71), who applies a similar five-point scale to measure the degree to which torture is practised across the globe. The scale is derived directly from the legal requirements found in the 1984 Convention against Torture and codes country practices based only on the US Department of State reports. Like the political terror scale, Hathaway uses a five-point scale that moves from no (or low) instances of torture (coded as 1) to widespread instances of torture (5). Table 5.7 shows the categories for coding the torture scale, where it is clear that each level contains a discrete set of practices, key words and decision rules for coding the narrative reports on torture found in the US Department of State reports. Hathaway (2002: 1,972) reports 80 per-cent agreement across her coding teams (Hathaway 2002: 1,972). While the scores were coded for the years 1985 to 1999, it is entirely possible for coding to be done on country reports for the years since 1999. The torture scale was originally used in Hathaway's (2002) analysis of the effectiveness of the inter-national rights regime and has featured in other cross-national and time-series analyses of human rights (see Landman 2005; Landman and Larizza 2009).

The political terror scale and the torture scale are directly comparable since they adopt the same five-point scale that is ordinal and interval, which is to say the scales are based on the assumptions that moving from one level down to another denotes a worse set of practices and that a move from a score of 2 to 3 is the same as a move from a score of 4 to 5. In other words, the increase in severity is the same in moving across the different levels of these scales. Torture, however, is but one type of human rights violation captured by the political terror scale, such that the two measures are comparable and show similar trends, but are not perfectly correlated with one another. For example, Figure 5.7 in Landman (2006a: 86) shows the trends in the two versions of the political scale for the period between 1976 and 2000 and the torture scale between 1985 and 1999, where it is clear that the trends do not fall into line until the mid-1990s. For the whole period, the overall correlation between the torture scale and the Amnesty version of the political terror scale is .61 ($p < .001$) and between the torture scale and the Department of State version of the political terror scale is .69 ($p < .001$).

Table 5.7 Torture scale levels

Level	Description
5	At least one of the following is true: Torture is 'prevalent' or 'widespread'; there is 'repeated' and 'methodical' torture; there are 'many' incidents of torture; torture is 'routine' or standard practice; torture is 'frequent'; there are 'common', 'frequent', or 'many' beatings to death or summary executions; or there are 'widespread' beatings to death
4	At least one of the following is true: Torture is 'common'; there are several reports of torture; there are 'many' or 'numerous' allegations of torture; torture is 'practised' (without reference to frequency); there is government apathy or ineffective prevention of torture; psychological punishment is 'frequently' or 'often' used; there are 'frequent' beatings or rough handling; 'occasional' incidents of beating to death; or there are 'several' reports of beatings to death
3	At least one of the following is true: There are 'some' or 'occasional' allegations of or incidents of torture (even 'isolated' incidents unless they have been redressed or are unsubstantiated (see above)); there are 'reports', 'allegations', or 'cases', of torture without reference to frequency; beatings are 'common' (or 'not uncommon'); there are 'isolated' incidents of beatings to death or summary executions (this includes unexplained deaths suspected to be attributed to brutality) or there are beatings to death or summary executions without reference to frequency; there is severe maltreatment of prisoners; there are 'numerous' reports of beatings; persons are 'often' subjected to beatings; there is 'regular' brutality; or psychological punishment is used
2	At least one of the following is true: There are only unsubstantiated and likely untrue allegations of torture; there are 'isolated' instances of torture for which the government has provided redress; there are allegations or indications of beatings, mistreatment or harsh/rough treatment; there are some incidents of abuse of prisoners or detainees; or abuse or rough treatment occurs 'sometimes' or 'occasionally'. Any reported beatings put a country into at least this category regardless of governmental systems in place to provide redress (except in the limited circumstances noted above)
1	There are no allegations or instances of torture in this year. There are no allegations or instances of beatings in this year; or there are only isolated reports of beatings by individual police officers or guards all of whom were disciplined when caught.

Source: Hathaway 2002: 1970–1971

Cingranelli and Richards (CIRI) human rights data

Drawing on these developments in the provision of standards-based measures of human rights, David Cingranelli and David Richards have assembled a large data set of measures for 13 different human rights for 195 countries for the period from 1980 to 2006, making this one of the most comprehensive cross-national time-series data collections on human rights in the world. The data comprise 0–2 scales for ten of the rights and 0–3 scales for three of the rights, where, in contrast to our previous examples of standards-based measures of human rights, a higher score denotes better government respect for the particular human right. Table 5.8 lists the rights that are included in the data set, the scores for the rights measures, their description and the criteria for assigning scores. Since its inception, the CIRI data have been coded using multiple teams and the project reports the inter-coder reliability tests as a matter of course.

Some of the separate scales are then used for aggregate indices, including a physical integrity rights index (ranging from 0 to 8) and an empowerment rights index (ranging from 0 to 10). The physical integrity rights index comprises a sum of scores for torture, extrajudicial killing, political imprisonment and disappearance. This selection of measures maps well onto the political terror scale, but since it aggregates separate measures, the contours and components that comprise it are more transparent to the analyst. Moreover, the separate indices can be examined alongside the aggregate index to see the ways in which particular rights violations drive an overall assessment and portrayal of physical integrity rights violations (see Figure 5.4). In similar fashion, the empowerment index combines the five separate measures for freedom of movement, freedom of speech, workers' rights, political participation and freedom of religion, which denote a general protection of those rights that allow for individual and collective expression and association, as well as participation in public affairs. Like the physical integrity rights index, analysis of the separate measures alongside the combined index yields additional insights into the types of human rights that are most important in driving the overall index (see Figure 5.5).

In addition to the collection of data, Cingranelli and Richards have developed a user-friendly and flexible web-based interface for creating data sets for download, as well as hosting the full documentation for the data. Users can specify the regions and countries, the number of variables and the years for which they need the data, which are then made available in Microsoft Excel and SPSS format. Like the other standards-based scales, the CIRI data can be used for global and regional comparisons, time-series mapping and single-country analysis across a wide range of human rights, including some economic and social rights relating to workers and women. Its inclusion of these latter set of rights makes the CIRI data project the first such project to provide standards-based measures of economic and social rights, and the first such project to take women's rights seriously.

Measuring the de jure human rights commitments of states

Standards-based scales can also be used to measure the *de jure* commitments that states make to the promotion and protection of human rights at both the domestic and international level. For the domestic level of national constitutions, scholars such Boli-Bennett (1976), Pritchard (1986), Hofrenning (1990), and Suksi (1993), Davenport (1996), Foweraker and Landman (1997), Cross (1999) and Keith (2002) have variously coded national constitutions across small and large samples of countries for descriptive analysis or to examine the

Table 5.8 Cingranelli and Richards (CIRI) human rights data

Human rights	Scores	Description	Coding rules
Extrajudicial killing	0–2	Extrajudicial killings are killings by government officials without due process of law. They include murders by private groups if instigated by government. These killings may result from the deliberate, illegal, and excessive use of lethal force by the police, security forces, or other agents of the state whether against criminal suspects, detainees, prisoners, or others.	A score of 0 indicates that extrajudicial killings were practiced frequently in a given year; a score of 1 indicates that extrajudicial killings were practiced occasionally; and a score of 2 indicates that such killings did not occur in a given year.
Disappearance	0–2	Disappearances are cases in which people have disappeared, political motivation appears likely, and the victims have not been found. Knowledge of the whereabouts of the disappeared is, by definition, not public knowledge. However, while there is typically no way of knowing where victims are, it is typically known by whom they were taken and under what circumstances.	A score of 0 indicates that disappearances have occurred frequently in a given year; a score of 1 indicates that disappearances occasionally occurred; and a score of 2 indicates that disappearances did not occur in a given year.
Torture	0–2	Torture refers to the purposeful inflicting of extreme pain, whether mental or physical, by government officials or by private individuals at the instigation of government officials. Torture includes the use of physical and other force by police and prison guards that is cruel, inhuman, or degrading. This also includes deaths in custody due to negligence by government officials.	A score of 0 indicates that torture was practiced frequently in a given year; a score of 1 indicates that torture was practiced occasionally; and a score of 2 indicates that torture did not occur in a given year.
Political imprisonment	0–2	Political imprisonment refers to the incarceration of people by government officials because of: their speech; their non-violent opposition to government policies or leaders; their religious beliefs; their non-violent religious practices including proselytizing; or their membership in a group, including an ethnic or racial group.	A score of 0 indicates that there were many people imprisoned because of their religious, political, or other beliefs in a given year; a score of 1 indicates that a few people were imprisoned; and a score of 2 indicates that no persons were imprisoned for any of the above reasons in a given year.

(continued on next page)

Table 5.8 (continued)

Human rights	Scores	Description	Coding rules
Freedom of speech	0–2	This variable indicates the extent to which freedoms of speech and press are affected by government censorship, including ownership of media outlets. Censorship is any form of restriction that is placed on freedom of the press, speech or expression. Expression may be in the form of art or music.	A score of 0 indicates that government censorship of the media was complete; a score of 1 indicates that there was some government censorship of the media; and a score of 2 indicates that there was no government censorship of the media in a given year.
Freedom of religion	0–1	This variable indicates the extent to which the freedom of citizens to exercise and practice their religious beliefs is subject to actual government restrictions. Citizens should be able to freely practice their religion and proselytize (attempt to convert) other citizens to their religion as long as such attempts are done in a non-coercive, peaceful manner.	A score of 0 indicates that the government restricted some religious practices, while a score of 1 indicates that the government placed no restrictions on religious practices in a year
Freedom of movement*	0–2	This variable indicates citizens' freedom to travel within their own country and to leave and return to that country.	A score of 0 indicates that domestic and foreign travel was restricted in a given year, while a score of 1 indicates that such travel was generally unrestricted.
Freedom of assembly and association	0–2	It is an internationally recognized right of citizens to assemble freely and to associate with other persons in political parties, trade unions, cultural organizations, or other special-interest groups. This variable indicates the extent to which the freedoms of assembly and association are subject to actual governmental limitations or restrictions (as opposed to strictly legal protections).	A score of 0 indicates that citizens' rights to freedom of assembly or association were severely restricted or denied completely to all citizens; a score of 1 indicates that these rights were limited for all citizens or severely restricted or denied for select groups; and a score of 2 indicates that these rights were virtually unrestricted and freely enjoyed by practically all citizens in a given year.
Electoral self-determination	0–2	This variable indicates to what extent citizens enjoy freedom of political choice and the legal right and ability in practice to change the laws and officials that govern them through free and fair elections. This right is sometimes known as the right to self-determination.	A score of 0 indicates that the right to self-determination through free and fair elections did not exist in law or practice during the year in question. A score of 1 indicates that while citizens had the legal right to self-determination, there were some limitations to the fulfilment of this right in practice. Therefore, in states receiving a 1, political participation was only moderately free and open. A score of 2 indicates that political participation was very free and open during the year in question and citizens had the right to self-determination through free and fair elections in both law and practice.

(continued on next page)

Table 5.8 (continued)

Human rights	Scores	Description	Coding rules
Workers' rights	0–2	Workers should have freedom of association at their workplaces and the right to bargain collectively with their employers. This variable indicates the extent to which workers enjoy these and other internationally recognized rights at work, including a prohibition on the use of any form of forced or compulsory labour; a minimum age for the employment of children; and acceptable conditions of work with respect to minimum wages, hours of work, and occupational safety and health.	A score of 0 indicates that workers' rights were severely restricted; a score of 1 indicates that workers' rights were somewhat restricted; and a score of 2 indicates that workers' rights were fully protected during the year in question.
Women's political rights	0–3	Women's political rights include a number of internationally recognized rights. These rights include: The right to vote The right to run for political office The right to hold elected and appointed government positions The right to join political parties The right to petition government officials	A score of 0 indicates that women's political rights were not guaranteed by law during a given year. A score of 1 indicates that women's political rights were guaranteed in law, but severely prohibited in practice. A score of 2 indicates that women's political rights were guaranteed in law, but were still moderately prohibited in practice. Finally, a score of 3 indicates that women's political rights were guaranteed in both law and practice.
Women's economic rights	0–3	Women's economic rights include a number of internationally recognized rights. These rights include: Equal pay for equal work Free choice of profession or employment without the need to obtain a husband or male relative's consent The right to gainful employment without the need to obtain a husband or male relative's consent Equality in hiring and promotion practices Job security (maternity leave, unemployment benefits, no arbitrary firing or layoffs, etc...) Non-discrimination by employers The right to be free from sexual harassment in the workplace The right to work at night The right to work in occupations classified as dangerous The right to work in the military and the police force	A score of 0 indicates that there were no economic rights for women in law and that systematic discrimination based on sex may have been built into law. A score of 1 indicates that women had some economic rights under law, but these rights were not effectively enforced. A score of 2 indicates that women had some economic rights under law, and the government effectively enforced these rights in practice while still allowing a low level of discrimination against women in economic matters. Finally, a score of 3 indicates that all or nearly all of women's economic rights were guaranteed by law and the government fully and vigorously enforces these laws in practice.

(continued on next page)

Table 5.8 (continued)

Human rights	Scores	Description	Coding rules
Women's social rights	0–3	Women's social rights include a number of internationally recognized rights. These rights include: The right to equal inheritance The right to enter into marriage on a basis of equality with men The right to travel abroad The right to obtain a passport The right to confer citizenship to children or a husband The right to initiate a divorce The right to own, acquire, manage, and retain property brought into marriage The right to participate in social, cultural, and community activities The right to an education The freedom to choose a residence/domicile Freedom from female genital mutilation of children and of adults without their consent Freedom from forced sterilization	A score of 0 indicates that there were no social rights for women in law and that systematic discrimination based on sex may have been built into law. A score of 1 indicates that women had some social rights under law, but these rights were not effectively enforced. A score of 2 indicates that women had some social rights under law, and the government effectively enforced these rights in practice while still allowing a low level of discrimination against women in economic matters. Finally, a score of 3 indicates that all or nearly all of women's social rights were guaranteed by law and the government fully and vigorously enforced these laws in practice.

Note:
* In 2007 this variable was split between Freedom of Domestic Movement and Freedom of International Movement.
Source: Adapted from ciri.binghamton.edu/documentation/ciri_variables_short_descriptions.pdf

degree to which formal commitment to human rights is related to actual protection of human rights. Across these studies, standardized scales are developed to award points to countries for the presence of constitutional provisions that explicitly address the protection of human and/or citizenship rights. Keith (2002: 125) provides an excellent example of how to code the *de jure* commitment of states at the domestic level. She identifies the following ten rights for coding: (1) freedom of speech, (2) freedom of association, (3) freedom of assembly, (4) freedom of the press, (5) freedom of religion, (6) the right to strike, (7) writ of habeas corpus, (8) the right to a public trial, (9) the right to a fair trial and (10) a ban on torture or other cruel and unusual punishment. Constitutional provisions for these rights are then coded as follows:

(2) explicit guarantee or mention in the constitution;
(1) explicit guarantee or mention in the constitution but notes exceptions or qualifications, such as a public interest clause;
(0) no mention in the constitution.

This coding scheme thus awards more points to those countries with more explicit protections provided in their constitutions, while providing a comparable set of scales that can be used separately or aggregated for the statistical analysis of a large sample of countries over time. While the set of rights provisions that have been coded are primarily civil and political rights protections, it is possible to expand the coding scheme to include other categories of human rights. For example, the 1988 Brazilian Constitution has many provisions within the realm of economic and social rights, which could be coded using Keith's (2002) scheme.

For the international level, it is possible to use similar schemes to code the *de jure* commitment of states to the promotion and protection of human rights. Such coding has been done for international environmental and financial regimes (see Mitchell 2000; Simmons 2000) and in the field of human rights scholars have begun devising methods for coding human rights treaty ratifications of countries. When a state accedes to a UN or regional human rights treaty (such as the European or American Conventions on Human Rights), it is obliged to file notification with the appropriate official international bodies. These bodies provide regularly updated listings of accessions, ratifications and reservations that have been entered by states, which provide primary source material for the assessment of state commitment to international human rights norms (see Office of the High Commissioner for Human Rights, www.unhchr.ch). Over the years, this primary information has formed the basis for coding schemes found in the United Nations Development Programme (UNDP) Human Development reports and in the global comparative studies, such as those carried out by Keith (1999), Hathaway (2002, 2003, 2007), Hafner-Burton (2005), Hafner-Burton and Tsutsui (2005), Landman (2005a), Neumayer (2005), Hafner-Burton, Tsutsui and Mayer (2008), and Vreeland (2008).

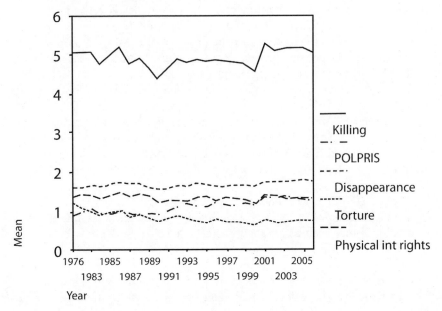

Figure 5.4 The four components and aggregate physical integrity rights index, 1980–2006
Source: CIRI data set

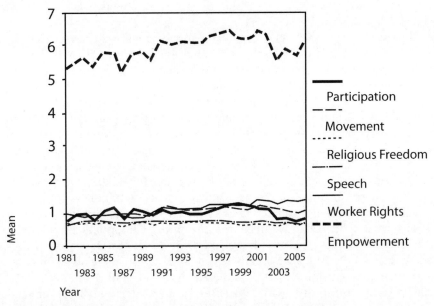

Figure 5.5 Five components and the empowerment index, 1980–2006
Source: CIRI data set

Across these studies, state ratification of international human rights treaties is coded using similar methods to those found in Keith's (2002) work on domestic constitutions. For example, Keith (1999) and Hathaway (2002) code the ratification of international human rights treaties using a dummy variable that assumes a value of 1 for ratification and 0 otherwise. Landman (2005a) codes countries with a 0 for no signature, 1 for signature and 2 for ratification. In order to reflect accurately the intent of states in making their formal commitments, Landman (2005a) devised an additional standards-based scale, which takes into account the degree to which states lodge reservations, or exceptions, to the content of the treaty to which they may have a particular objection given their own legal culture or legal system. For example, the USA made a reservation to the death penalty when it signed the International Covenant on Civil and Political Rights (ICCPR) (Malanczuk 1997: 135; see also Sherman 1994), since the jurisdiction over the death penalty is left to the individual states in the US federal system. According to Article 2 (1) (d) of the *Vienna Convention on the Law of Treaties*, a reservation is a unilateral statement made by a state that 'purports to exclude or to modify the legal effect of certain provisions of the treaty in their application to that State' (cited in Malanczuk 1997: 135; see also Brownlie 2003: 584–87). Each reservation variable rewards countries for making no reservations to a treaty upon ratification and punishes them in varying degrees for making reservations upon ratification. The scale codes reservations using the following four categories:

(4) *Given to countries that have no reservations with regard to said treaty, interpretive declarations that do not modify obligations, or non-substantial declarations.* This would include declarations such as criticism of the treaty not being open to all states, or political non-recognition of other states.
(3) *Given to countries whose reservations could have some but not major impact on their obligations.* This would include reservations to certain aspects of a specific right but not nullifying it completely. Or to whole articles that are procedural (such as articles allowing one-sided referral to the International Court of Justice, ICJ).
(2) *Given to countries whose reservations have noticeable effect on their obligations under the treaty to a whole article, nullifying or leaving open the possibility not to abide by a whole article.* This score would also be given for reservations that do not limit a whole right or article, but nevertheless contain the core obligation of the article or right.
(1) *Given to countries whose reservations can have significant and severe effects on the treaty obligations.* This would include reservations that show disregard for the object and purpose, or for rules of customary international law. Reservations that subject the whole treaty to national or religious legislation would receive this score.

By rewarding countries for not having reservations, it is possible to multiply the two separate types of variables (ratification and reservation) to produce a third type of *weighted* ratification variable that takes into account a country's initial intent at the time of ratification. The following hypothetical example helps clarify the differences among these three types of treaty variables:

> *State A ratifies ICCPR in 1985 with no reservations:*
> [ICCPR ratification = 2]*[ICCPR reservation = 4] = [weighted ratification variable = 8]

> *State B ratifies ICCPR in 1985 with serious reservations:*
> [ICCPR ratification = 2]*[ICCPR reservation = 1] = [weighted ratification variable = 2]

   The combination of the ratification variable and the reservation variable in this example produces a weighted ratification variable, which changes fundamentally the depiction and meaning of the overall pattern of ratifications. Without the weighting variable, State A and State B would be indistinguishable in terms of their formal commitment to the ICCPR. The addition of the weighting variable 'discounts' the ratification variable for State B since it had serious reservations that undermined the object and purpose of the treaty. While both states are 'rewarded' for ratifying the ICCPR, State B is 'punished' for having serious reservations. The different scales for ratification and weighted ratification can be analysed over time and space to show differences in state behaviour. The time-series plot in Figure 5.6 shows that as more and more states ratified treaties between 1976 and 2000 they did so with fewer reservations, a trend that became more marked after the collapse of the Soviet Union and the 1989 velvet revolutions. The regional comparisons in Figure 5.7 show that communist and post-communist European countries had lower rates of ratification with fewer reservations, while Western European countries had higher rates of ratification with more reservations. Outside of Europe, rates of ratification are significantly lower, particularly in South Asia and East Asia and the Pacific, but with fewer reservations. These and other descriptive inferences are possible with such coding of ratification and reservation behaviour of states, while second order analysis can examine empirical relationships between the law and practice of human rights.

Uses and limitations of standards-based measures

Standards-based measures of human rights have become a dominant feature of social scientific analysis, particularly in the fields of political science and international relations. Since the first cross-national statistical analysis on human rights in the late 1980s (Mitchell and McCormick 1988), there has been a proliferation of studies using increasingly large and complex data sets and an expanding list of independent variables in which standards-based measures of human rights feature across most of the studies as a key dependent variable (see Landman 2005a, 2008, 2009; Moore 2006). The independent variables

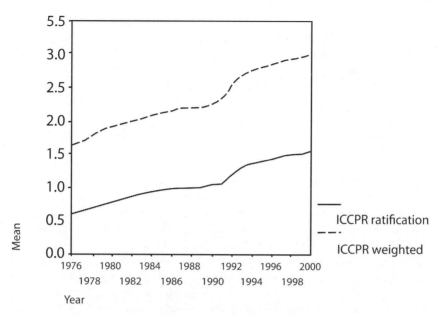

Figure 5.6 Mean ratification and weighted ratification measures of the 1966 *International Covenant on Civil and Political Rights*, 1976–2000

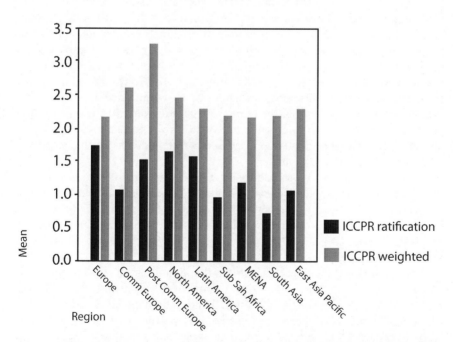

Figure 5.7 Mean ratification and weighted ratification measures of the 1966 *International Covenant on Civil and Political Rights* across regions, 1976-2000

have most notably included the level, pace and quality of economic development (e.g. Henderson 1991; Poe and Tate 1994; Poe et al. 1999); the level, timing and quality of democratization (e.g. Davenport 1999; Zanger 2000b; Davenport and Armstrong 2004; Bueno de Mesquita et al. 2005); involvement in internal and external conflict (Poe and Tate 1994; Poe et al. 1999); the size and growth of the population (Henderson 1993; Poe and Tate 1994; Poe et al. 1999); the level of global interdependence (Landman 2005b); and the growth and effectiveness of international human rights law (Keith 1999; Hathaway 2002; Landman 2005b; Neumayer 2005; Hafner-Burton and Tsutsui 2005; Hafner-Burton et al. 2008; Vreeland 2008). Where human rights feature as an independent variable, studies have primarily examined how the variation in human rights protection is related to the foreign direct investment and/or the presence of multinationals (Meyer 1996, 1998, 1999a, 1999b; Smith et al. 1999) and structural adjustment programmes (SAPs) implemented by the World Bank and the International Monetary Fund (IMF) (see Abouharb and Cingranelli 2007).

The comparable, standard and time-series nature of these measures has made them particularly popular in social science research projects that seek to make empirical generalizations across a large sample of countries and time. The effort in such projects is to test empirical theories and build statistical models that explain the variation in human rights protection, while remaining attentive to regional variation and anomalous cases that do not conform to theoretical expectations (Landman 2003, 2008). The findings are by definition general in nature and involve statements such as 'countries with a large population have worse records at protecting human rights'; 'democracies are better at protecting human rights than non-democracies'; 'there is a significant but limited impact of the international law of human rights on the human rights practices of states'; and 'human rights practices of recipient states matter for the initial decision to offer a structural adjustment programme, but that during the period of implementation, the human rights situation in the recipient states got worse'. In all these examples, the statement involves a relationship between an explanatory variable (population, democracy, international law and structural adjustment) and human rights.

Despite the popularity and increasing use of standards-based measures of human rights, there are a significant number of limitations to them that centre on questions of their source material, limited set of human rights, the national aggregation problem and what is called 'variance truncation' (see Landman and Häusermann 2003; UNDP 2006). Freedom House uses a mixture of source material from foreign and domestic newspapers and news reports, academic analyses, non-governmental organizations, think thanks, individual professional contacts and visits to the regions. One version of the political terror scale, the torture scale, and the Cingranelli and Richards human rights scores all use the annual Country Reports from the US Department of State, while the second version of the political terror scale uses annual Country Reports from Amnesty International. Across these examples, there is a trade-off between consistency and bias. Where Freedom House uses a mix of sources to arrive at a 'mean' account, there is very little transparency offered as to the precise mix of sources, their number and the ways in which pieces of information ultimately are used to yield a country score for any given year. It does not use multiple coding teams and, therefore, cannot test for inter-coder reliability. The other scales gain a certain consistency in the use of the same sources and enhance their reliability through the use of multiple coding teams and inter-coder reliability tests, but suffer from the inherent biases associated with an over-reliance on too few sources. The political terror scale does, however, code from two different sources and thus offers a set of checks on its portrayal of human rights conditions around the world. However, none of the standards-based scales involve the meticulous coding procedures and multiple systems approach used in the generation of events-based data discussed in the previous chapter, illustrating one of the many trade-offs between and among validity, reliability and comprehensive coverage of countries.

The second limitation to standards-based measures involves their focus on a fairly limited set and single dimension of human rights. Freedom House, the political terror scale and the torture scale all provide measures for the respect dimension of civil and political rights and ultimately focus on state responsibility for human rights protection. Part of this focus is methodological and part is ideological. Methodologically, these sets of rights appeal to the intuitive sense of rights 'violations' by the state, imply a degree of variation in such violations and allow a score to be assigned to the relative severity of the violations, which yields the kinds of scales that have been discussed here. Ideologically, the generation of these scales has been done by organizations and individuals based in the USA, which historically has placed more emphasis on the primary and 'fundamental' nature of civil and political rights as 'core' rights, versus the less important sets of economic and social rights. Such a distinction and privileging of these rights follows a longer liberal tradition in the theory of citizenship rights (see Foweraker and Landman 1997, 2000; Landman 2005a). In their development of scales for workers' rights and women's economic and social rights, Cingranelli and Richards have broken new ground in the field of standards-based measures of human rights.

Thirdly, as we saw in the previous chapter on events-based measures, human rights violations show a tremendous amount of sub-national variation in terms of the number of violations, the main perpetrators and the profiles of the main victims. Moreover, the explanations for such sub-national variation rely on a set of factors that also vary sub-nationally, such as income inequality, urban-rural differences, ethnic composition and fractionalization, differences in terrain, and differences in the possibility for the collective use of political violence (see, in particular Ball et al. 2003; and also Kalyvas 2006; Landman and Larizza 2009). None of the measures discussed in this chapter capture such sub-national variation. Rather, each country-year in these data sets receives a single score, which represents a general impression or picture of the human rights situation in the country. This means that a particularly harsh situation in one part of the country owing to armed or ethnic conflict could lower an overall score for that country in a given year, and such scores would say very little about the types of people who are more likely to suffer human rights abuses. Like the other limitations, the national aggregation problem represents a further trade-off between the cross-national comparability of a measure and the country-specific information that it represents.

Finally, the use of limited ordinal and interval scales for measuring human rights brings with it the problem of 'variance truncation'. It is clear that there is great variation in the protection of human rights around the world and, more importantly, practices among the worst human rights performers show tremendous variation, as do those among the best human rights performers. Coding all countries on a limited scale means that much of that variation is simply lost or 'truncated' into the various categories of the scale. For example, Cingranelli and Richards code their scale for extra-judicial killings as follows:

(0)   If there are more than 50 political killings in any given year;
(1)   If there are between 1 and 49 political killings in any given year;
(2)   If there are no political killings in any given year.

Now, imagine a country that has 52 political killings in a year and a country that has 50,000 killings in a year. Under the CIRI system, both countries receive a score of 0, meaning that it is impossible to make any distinction between these two countries for that year, even though one has significantly more political killings than the other. Equally, imagine one Organisation for Economic Co-operation and Development (OECD) country that experiences two political killings and one that experiences 48 killings. As before, both countries would receive the same score of 1 under this system, making it impossible to distinguish between two OECD countries, a problem that has been addressed through the use of additional forms of data (see Foweraker and Krznaric 2003). In both hypothetical examples, however, we thus see a tremendous loss of information, which reduces down a natural variation in human rights abuse into a limited set of categories.

These various limitations suggest that only certain types of general analysis can be conducted with them and that caution be exercised in drawing any inferences beyond those with a general applicability. The measures outlined in this chapter do provide comparability, comprehensive spatial and temporal coverage, and generate annual scores on a regular basis. However, they are not particularly good for single-country analysis as the between-unit variation in the scales is often much greater than the within-unit variation; in other words, the scales are a reasonable way with which to make general comparisons and identify large differences between countries, but for many countries the scores do not change significantly over time, unless the country is undergoing significant political change owing to a democratic transition, military coup, foreign occupation or other event that brings with it a change in the human rights situation.

6   Survey-based measures

Introduction

The past two chapters discussed the generation, design, use and limitations of events-based measures and standards-based measures of human rights. This chapter follows suit by examining survey-based measures, the definitive features of which are their use of a large sample of individuals (usually selected randomly) who answer a set of predefined questions about either their *perceptions* of human rights or their *experiences* of human rights within their own country. As we showed in Chapter 4, many examples of events-based measures use some sort of narrative provided by a *deponent*, who provides a direct account of human rights violations that he or she has experienced, witnessed, or has knowledge about from accounts from family members, friends and neighbours, or other related individuals. The task of the analyst is to code the account after the statement has been taken. We also saw in Chapter 4 that the individuals who come forward as deponents are not random, but represent a 'convenience' sample against which particular statistical methods are used to alleviate the worst forms of bias that result from the use of such samples. In contrast, survey-based measures typically design some sort of survey instrument that comprises set questions with limited response categories, which are coded as the respondent answers the questions to the survey. Additionally, the selection of respondents is random, such that the analyst can use standard inferential statistics (see Box 6.1) to make meaningful statements about general human rights conditions relevant to the target population under examination. The key differences between the two methods are that survey-based measures use *respondents* instead of *deponents* and *random* instead of *non-random* samples.

The survey instrument has been the work horse of the social sciences, polling organizations, market research firms and analysts seeking to tap into the thoughts, perceptions, preferences, intentions and experiences of individuals since the early years of the 20th century (see Weisberg 2005: 1–16). Academic institutions have long-term funded projects on individuals and households, which use survey instruments to measure their voting preferences (e.g. the American National Election Studies and the British Election Studies); life choices, work–life balance issues, social attitudes and habits (British Social

Box 6.1 Survey samples and standard inferential statistics

Survey research is grounded in the use of *random samples*. A random sample is also known as a *probability sample*, which means that within a population, each individual has an equal chance of being selected as part of the sample. If this is the case and the sample is relatively large, then it has a number of properties that allow for the analyst to make *inferences* from the sample to the population as a whole. Survey analysts are most interested in the percentage of people within a sample that give responses to questions and whether that percentage is an accurate reflection of the percentage response were a survey to be given to the whole population. The accuracy of the calculation of these percentages is a direct function of the sample size, such that accuracy increases with larger samples. For example, if an analyst wanted to be 95 percent confident in the calculation of percentage response in the population, with 3 percent margin of error, then a sample of 1,100 people from the population would be sufficient. Using such a sample would allow the following kind of statement to be made:

'We are 95 percent confident that the proportion of the population that agrees that the human rights situation has deteriorated in the last five years is 25 percent, plus or minus 3 percent.'

The real percentage of the population that agrees that the human rights situation has deteriorated is somewhere between 22 percent and 28 percent. The range of values (in this case 6 percent between 22 and 28) would be bigger if a smaller sample of people were used or smaller if a larger sample of people were used. For human rights research, particularly in countries with the presence of different ethnic and religious minority groups, the generation of samples becomes more complicated in order for a fair representation of the different groups that comprise society to be achieved. In general, however, the use of random samples and survey techniques has aided in the analysis of perceptions and experiences of human rights that apply to the whole population.

Attitudes and The British Household Panel Survey); policy preferences, feelings, support for democracy and citizen engagement (e.g. the World Barometer and its associated regional variants, such as the Eurobarometer, Latinobarometro and Afrobarometer); and general perceptions and commitments to different sets of values (e.g. the World Values Survey). Like these more notable examples, human rights scholars and practitioners adopt the same basic methodology and use survey instruments to gauge the perceptions and measure the human rights experiences of individuals. The responses from individuals in the sample to the survey questions are then used to make inferences about the human rights situation in all or part of the country either for the time period in which the survey was conducted or in retrospect to periods of time in the past. For example, Physicians for Human Rights, a non-governmental organization based in Cambridge, Massachusetts, USA has carried out retrospective surveys on sexual violence in Sierra Leone (see Physicians for Human Rights 2002) and the Commission on Reception, Truth and Reconciliation Timor-Leste (CAVR) used a survey of households from which retrospective family mortality histories were collected (see below and Silva and Ball 2006: 8).

As in all of our examples of human rights measures, there are strengths and weaknesses associated with survey-based methods for human rights measurement. Without careful attention to all the stages in carrying out a survey, significant kinds of errors can taint the process and lead to potential biases in the measurement and analysis of human rights. To address these concerns, this chapter first discusses the fundamental issues surrounding *survey design*, *sampling decisions* and the *use of inferential statistics* in making estimations about the whole population from a sample. The discussion is illustrated with examples of survey-based measures of human rights from the academic, non-governmental and truth commission sectors working in the field of human rights. It concludes with a discussion of the limitations of survey-based measures of human rights, including issues surrounding low response rates, forced responses, timidity and misinformation, absence of voice in providing a human rights assessment or account, and their 'snapshot' nature.

The familiarity of surveys

Although many of us are highly familiar with surveys, either having had experience as a respondent ourselves or having read and worked with the results of surveys carried out on many different topics, there are significant challenges in designing a survey that will capture the meaning of the concept, problem, or idea that is meant to be measured and will allow the data that have been collected to be analysed in a way that provides a useful tool for making generalizations about a particular context or situation under examination. Survey research goes through a series of stages from the original specification of the research question and problem to the final analysis and publication of the results. Table 6.1 shows the 12 key stages in any survey project, the scope and meaning of these stages and what they mean for the measurement of human rights using survey instruments. It is clear from the table that careful attention is required at each stage of the process in order to avoid or minimize errors that reduce the ability of the survey to measure human rights in ways that are valid, meaningful and reliable. The fundamental aspects of a survey project that are of particular importance here involve survey design, sampling and inferences. The design of the survey instrument itself includes the type, number, style and ordering of questions, as well as the kind of interviewing strategy that is employed. The sampling frame and sampling strategy are related to the objectives of the research and the context under which the survey will be administered. The types of inferences that are made possible from the combination

Table 6.1 Stages in the survey research process as applied to human rights

Stage in survey project	Scope and meaning	Application to human rights
1 Identify research objectives	What is the objective of the project? What does the project hope to learn? What topic or topics are included?	Area of human rights or particular human rights focus Specific human rights Rights-based issues of some kind

2 Identify the target population	The group to which inferences are to be made	Whole population
		Particular groups
		    Women
		    Ethnic minorities
		    Internally displaced people
		    Elderly
		    Children
		    Poor

3 Choose the mode and design of the survey	Type of interviewing
	    Face to face
	    Phone
	    Mail
	    Internet
	Design
	    Closed questions
	    Open questions
		Special issues with human rights suggest that face to face interviews are preferred
		A mixture of open and closed questions are preferred to give extra flexibility for capturing complexity of a human rights perception or experience

4 Choose the sampling frame	A list or other record of the population from which the sample will be drawn	Careful attention is needed here, especially for those contexts in which lists of individuals or households are non-existent, incomplete, biased, or manipulated in some way.

Table 6.1 (continued)

Stage in survey project	Scope and meaning	Application to human rights

5 Choose the sampling method	Random (probability samples)
	  Simple
	  Stratified
	  Systematic
	  Cluster
	Non-Random
	  Availability samples
	    Convenience
	    Volunteer
	  Purposive samples
	    Typical
	    Critical
	    Snowball
	  Quota samples
		Random samples in human rights will necessarily yield low 'hit rates' in which respondents report on human rights experiences
		Extant human rights survey projects tend to use random samples of smaller target populations, such as internally displaced people

6 Write the questions	Question wording Response wording and coding Question ordering	Crucial aspect of any survey project and vital for a human rights survey with reflection on categories, dimensions, and meanings of rights
7 Train interview teams	Local teams with language abilities Develop empathy and rapport with target population	The sensitivity of human rights survey research requires special attention to rapport between interview staff and respondents
8 Pre-test the questionnaire	Pilot study with small sample of respondents	Even more important for human rights research in order to gauge response rates and data quality
9 Recruit respondents	Draw the sample and invite respondents to be interviewed	
10 Ask questions	Interview the respondents	

Table 6.1 (continued)

Stage in survey project	Scope and meaning	Application to human rights
11 Process data	Look for missing data Code open ended questions	A key component of this stage is to identify inconsistencies in response and to have multiple coding teams, especially for open ended questions

12 Analyse the data	Run descriptive summaries
	Bivariate analysis
	  cross-tabulations
	  correlations
	Multivariate analysis
	Regression
		Look for distributions and patterns in response across questions on human rights
		Establish associations between attributes of respondents and human rights perceptions and experiences, as well as significant 'between-group' differences (although hard to do with relatively small samples)

Source: adapted from Weisberg (2005: 17); Vogt (1999).

of the design, sampling frame and sample give the whole project meaning, in the sense that the goal of any human rights measurement project is to make larger inferences about a particular human rights situation in a given country context.

Survey design

As in events-based and standards-based measurement efforts, survey-based methods seek to provide valid, meaningful and reliable measures of human rights through converting our conceptual understanding of human rights into a quantitative score of some kind. In events-based and standards-based measures, some sort of human rights narrative is coded *after the fact*; giving numerical expression to a qualitative account based on a detailed story from a single deponent or an amalgam of different stories from a variety of sources. In contrast, most survey-based measures code the human rights information *before* the interview, where the different questions comprising the survey provide important cues to the respondent that elicit his or her understanding of particular human rights 'facts' as they relate to the question. It had been a long-held view that survey instruments are based on the assumption that respondents hold relatively well-formed views, sets of experiences, or perceptions and attitudes about the particular topic the survey is meant to tap (see, e.g. Zaller and Feldman 1992). More recently, however, psephologists and public opinion researchers have come to believe that individuals 'carry around in their heads a mix of only partially consistent ideas and considerations' and that any ideas that are uncovered through survey techniques are highly susceptible to the context in which questions are asked, the order in which the questions and their responses are listed, and the ways in which questions are worded (Ibid., 579.). These insights are equally (if not more) applicable to human rights research and analysis, and suggest that any design element in survey-based measures of human rights needs to pay close attention to the interview context, question wording, question ordering, and response categories and ordering.

The first step in a survey-based project on human rights is to understand the definitions and main parameters of the human rights that are to be measured. Concepts are mental categories (Buckingham and Saunders 2004: 63) and survey design is meant to probe the individual's understanding of these categories, experiences in their lives that relate to them and perceptions they might have about them. Any questions that probe an individual's experience or perception of human rights needs to pay attention to significant questions of validity. First, does the question (or questions) have what is called 'face validity', which is to say, does the question adequately capture the meaning of the particular human right 'on the face of it'? Second, does the question (or questions) have content validity, where all dimensions of the human right are covered by the questions? Third, does the question (or questions) achieve internal validity, where responses across batteries of related questions on the human right are logically consistent? Finally, does the question (or questions) provide for external validity, where responses simply appear to contradict other known information about the respondent? (Ibid. 65). Clearly, questions about direct experiences of human rights abuse are different from those probing general perceptions of the human rights situation, but question wording, response options and numbering, and question order are all crucial for establishing these different kinds of validity.

There are a number of general rules of thumb that apply to the design of questions and the type of wording that they use. These include (Buckingham and Saunders 2004: 76–85):

1 learning from previous research to avoid particular pitfalls;
2 keeping questions simple and unambiguous;
3 avoiding leading questions that bias the response in some way;
4 ordering questions in ways that do not influence later responses;
5 asking specific and concrete questions that actually have an answer; and
6 providing a sensible layout of the questionnaire, including the instructions to the respondent through the survey instrument.

These rules of thumb can be illustrated in part through reference to an existing study, which compares perceptions of human rights using survey-based measures to human rights practices using standards-based measures (i.e. Freedom House and the political terror scale) across 17 countries in East-Central Europe (Anderson et al. 2005). The section of the analysis that rests on survey-based measures discusses the concept of human rights, offers a minimal definition (i. e. personal integrity rights violations), and then allows room for the fact that 'it is simply not known whether citizens follow such a minimalist definition of *human rights* when forming evaluations of their country's human rights conditions' (Ibid.: 774, emphasis in the original). The article uses individual-level survey data collected on random samples of approximately 1,000 respondents, collected as part of the Central and Eastern Eurobarometer Study No. 7.[1] The key question on human rights in the survey was worded as follows (Anderson et al. 2005: 779):

'How much respect is there for individual human rights nowadays in your country? Do you feel that there is a lot of respect, some respect, not much respect, or no respect at all?'

The response categories are then coded in a scale ranging from 1 (no respect at all) to 4 (a lot of respect), which provides an ordinal measure of the perception of human rights that awards more points to the individual perception that rights are better respected within the country. For the countries in the study, the mean response is 2.16 with a standard deviation of .84 (Anderson et al. 2005: 796), which in other words means that across the sample of individuals in these countries there is a general perception that ranges from *not much respect* to *some respect*. The perception of highest respect for rights is obtained in Hungary (2.49) and the lowest in Russia (1.62), where roughly half of the respondents in Russia and Ukraine reported that there was no respect for human rights (Ibid.: 780–81).

In this example, the perception of human rights is captured by one question that has significant face validity, since it refers directly to human rights, focuses on the respect for individual rights rather than group rights, and allows for a range of responses that vary from negative to positive evaluations of the situation (Anderson et al. 2005: 779, fn. 3). The question does not, however, define human rights for the respondent. Rather, the respondent is meant to tap into his or her own understanding of human rights, compare their own understanding of rights to their perception of the respect for human rights in their country, and then respond using the four categories of evaluation available to them. There are, thus, conceptual and methodological limitations to the way in which this particular question and its responses have been designed, and there are limits to the comparability of the measure since it is not clear that respondents within and between countries have the same or equivalent understanding of human rights (see Sartori 1970; MacIntyre 1971; Mayer 1989; Van Deth 2009). First, the question does not ask about particular human rights categories (i.e. civil, political, economic, social and/or cultural), nor does it ask about particular human rights violations (e.g. the right to a fair trial, the right not to be tortured, freedom of association, the right to health, etc.). This means the respondent is free to think about any kinds of human rights and the degree to which he or she thinks they are protected within their country. Second, the respondent is given a limited set of response categories ranging only from 1 (no respect at all) to 4 (a lot of respect), leading to a similar problem of variance truncation that affects standards-based measures (see Chapter 5). It is entirely possible for respondents to have great variability in response to this general question about human rights, but they are only provided with four categories to register their perception. One solution is to use a 'feeling thermometer' of some kind that allows the respondent to register his or her perception on a scale that ranges from 1 to 100. While this alleviates some of the problem, all measurement strategies encounter this general limitation and in analysing the resulting data, it might be the case that responses 'cluster' within certain sections of the range and can be reduced down further anyway. The general rule of thumb, however, is to provide a good range of response and to avoid a 'forced' response as much as possible.

Sampling

The second element in the design and use of survey-based measures of human rights involves the selection of a sample from which meaningful and secure inferences can be drawn. One of the foundations of survey research in general is the reliance on a selected sample that has some correspondence to the target population that a survey seeks to address. Developments in inferential statistics have shown that relatively small random samples drawn from the target population can be analysed in ways that provide meaningful measures of attitudes, opinions and perceptions that apply to the whole target population. A random sample is one in which every individual in a population has an equal and independent chance of being selected for the study (see, e.g. Tashakkori and Teddlie 1998). The question surrounding the representativeness of such a sample centres on two key points: (1) the sample size and (2) the variance of the variable that is being measured (Weisberg 2005: 225–31). If the sample is small and the variance is high, then the sample is likely not to be representative, while if the sample is large and the variance is small, then the sample is more likely to be representative. The underlying assumption behind this logic is that as the sample size increases, the distribution of the variable of interest and its associated attributes (i.e. its mean, mode and standard deviation) approaches the distribution and attributes of that variable in the target population. For example, if a project wanted to know the average age of students at a particular university, a sample of 1,000 students will yield a closer approximation than a sample of just 50 students, since the 1,000-person sample has more observations and the distribution of the variable (in this case age) would approach a normal distribution with a set of attributes that more closely represent the attributes of the distribution of the target population (i.e. the whole population of the university). Statistical research has shown, however, that there are decreasing marginal returns to using ever-larger sample sizes, since the gains in accuracy in using larger samples become smaller as the sample size increases. This is why most public opinion surveys are happy to use samples of 1,500 to 2,000 respondents, where the relevant statistics that are calculated come with associated margins of error that reflect the sample size. It is important to stress, however, that these relationships between sample size, distributions, attributes and inferences are only relevant when a project employs random samples.

The link between the sample population and the target population is no different in efforts to use surveys to measure human rights, but there are some additional sampling problems that need to be overcome when employing the survey method to measure human rights. First, surveys that measure general perceptions of human rights such as the Eurobarometer survey discussed above can easily use random (or probability) samples drawn from an appropriate sampling frame. Surveys that seek to measure direct experiences of human rights violations, however, face an additional problem related to samples, since the proportion of the population that has actually experienced a violation of human rights is relatively small. The solution to this problem has been to use some kind of non-probability sample, such as purposely focusing on a group that is likely to have had experiences with human rights violations and then limit the inferences that are drawn to that target population. For example, in its research on violence against women in Afghanistan during Taliban rule, Physicians for Human Rights (1998: 43) used a random sample of 54 female heads of household who had lived in Kabul at least two years before 1996, which was complemented with 26 additional participants through snowball sampling identified through discussions with humanitarian organizations. The results of the study are not generalizable to all women in Afghanistan, but nonetheless revealed a telling portrait about their human rights experiences during that period.

Second, much human rights research focuses on the differences in perceptions and experiences across various groups in society, such as women, ethnic and religious minorities, indigenous groups and the poor, among many other categories of social identity. Sample sizes necessarily have to be very large in order to capture significant numbers of people from each of these groups. For example, the Bangladesh Bureau of Statistics carries out a regular survey of 10,000 households, but the sample size is not large enough to capture the more than 40 different religious and ethnic minority groups that comprise the population.[2] One solution is to enlarge the samples to capture these different groups, but such a solution is costly and may not be possible in lesser-developed countries, precisely where such data are greatly needed and relevant for human rights scholars and practitioners. Indeed, there is heavy donor demand for disaggregated indicators on various aspects of human rights, but there are real and significant issues surrounding the cost of implementing survey projects that require such large samples to capture the different groups that make up society. The second solution to this problem is to focus on only one or a few groups and limit the inferences that are drawn to that target population. Again, Physicians for Human Rights provides a good example. In their research on sexual violence in Sierra Leone, they interviewed 991 female heads of household from a population of internally displaced people about retrospective experiences of sexual violence and other human rights abuses, the inferences from which relate to other internally displaced women, but not to other women or the population as a whole (Physicians for Human Rights 2002: 37–39).

Third, surveys conducted in peaceful countries with well-developed infrastructure, phone registries and other demographic information have little difficulty in the choice of a sampling frame or the generation of random samples from which inferences can be made to the target population. However, conducting such surveys in war-torn countries, post-conflict societies, newly independent states, or new democracies after prolonged periods of authoritarian rule poses additional challenges for researchers. In many such contexts, there are no population registers or other sampling frames, broken down or non-existent infrastructure, no census data and other demographic data, and the population is in constant flux, either returning from displacement and exile, or moving about between old, renovated and/or new homes. Bosnia and Herzegovina (BiH) after the civil war between 1992 and 1995 that followed the breakup of the former Yugoslavia presents such a context (see Lynn 2003). Though not a human rights survey, the Household Budget Survey 2003 (HBS) provides an example in which some of these challenges were overcome to provide a useful random sample from which meaningful inferences could be drawn. The HBS was designed in response to particular inefficiencies that were found in an earlier study, the Living Standards Measurement Survey 2001 (LSMS). The HBS adopted an 'area-based' approach, which is a three-stage process of selecting what were known as 'enumeration areas' based on equal probability, then conducting field research to count the number of dwellings in each enumeration area, and then selecting an equal-probability sample of dwellings from that list. The biggest challenge was in the listing of dwellings, which used a 'semi-intrusive' approach, which required face-to-face interviewing. After a field test and full implementation of the HBS, the sampling strategy proved to be more efficient than the strategy employed in the LSMS and serves as a sampling technique for contexts with features that are similar to those confronted in Bosnia and Herzegovina (Lynn 2003: 29–30). In contrast to events-based data of the kind used by truth commissions, where no random samples are likely, this areas-based approach is a good method for generating a random sample, but there are still the remaining challenges for human rights researchers in getting meaningful responses using survey methods.

Inferences

The final and related element in the use of surveys concerns the type of information that is actually gathered and the types of inferences that are made possible through using surveys. There are numbers generated that relate to the *sample population* only and those that relate to the *target population*. For example, in our example above regarding the perception of human rights in Eastern Europe, respondents in Hungary registered a mean response of 2.49 (Anderson et al. 2005: 781), which is somewhat higher toward the category of 'greater respect' of human rights on the scale from 1 to 4. However, it is a *mean* response across the sample of Hungarians, where respondents expressed their perceptions across the full range of categories. Indeed, 14.4 percent of the respondents registered that human rights were not at all respected, 29.6 percent said that respect for human rights was 'not much', 48.7 percent said 'some' respect, and only 7.1 percent said that there was 'a lot' of respect for human rights (Ibid.: 781). Moreover, the perception of 'some' respect for human rights was expressed by the largest proportion of respondents and, with a typical margin of error of plus or minus 3 percent[3,] one could say that roughly between 45 and 51 percent of Hungarians claim that there is 'some' respect for human rights. The range of percentages and the precise margin of error is a direct function of the sample size, where the larger the sample size, the smaller the margin of error.

The numbers that are achieved by analysing a sample of the target population are thus merely estimates that approach the *true* values in the target population. Thus, by definition they come with an associated margin of error. In more general terms, survey analysis of human rights perceptions and experiences can take the following form:

1 N percent (±SE) of people in country X believe that human rights are not well respected;
2 N percent (±SE) of people in country X believe that human rights are well respected;
3 N percent (±SE) of people in country X have been a victim of a human rights violation(s);
4 N percent (±SE) of people in country X know a victim of a human rights violation(s).

In these examples, 1 and 2 are perceptions of the human rights situation in a particular country, such as in the examples discussed above, while 3 and 4 are actually experiences of human rights. The first two examples of response would result from a scale of the kind adopted in the Eurobarometer studies discussed above, while the latter two would result from a binary coding of questions on each type of violation experienced (e.g. 1 = 'yes', 0 = 'no'). These response examples are known as *univariate statistics*, since they report only the results on one variable, in this case either perception or experience of human rights. Such univariate statistics can be further analysed and broken down across groups, such as gender, religious and ethnic minority status, rural and urban locations, levels of education, levels of income, and other categories of social identity that might be of interest to a human rights project. In this case, the general form of inferences would look as follows:

5 N percent (±SE) of women in country X believe that human rights are not well respected (with inferential statistic);
6 N percent (±SE) of the indigenous population in country X believe that human rights are well respected (with inferential statistic);
7 N percent (±SE) of men under the age of 25 in country X have been a victim of a human rights violation(s) (with inferential statistic);
8 N percent (±SE) of women in country X know a victim of a human rights violation(s) (with inferential statistic);
9 N percent (±SE) of women in country X suffered arbitrary detention (with inferential statistic);
10 N percent (±SE) of the indigenous population in country X suffered torture (with inferential statistic);
11 N percent (±SE) of people in country X had been tortured by a rebel group (with inferential statistic).

In these examples, it is typical for the analyst to run what are called *cross-tabulations* and examine either the number or percentage of respondents that fall into the various categories. For example, a cross-tabulation between gender and arbitrary detention would compare the percentage of respondents who are women and have been detained arbitrarily to the percentage of respondents that are men and have been detained (and vice versa). In addition, such an analysis also calculates whether the differences between groups (in this case men and women) that are observed are statistically significant, and how much of the variation in the detention variable is due to the gender of the respondent (i.e. the 'goodness of fit'). Statistical software packages such as SPSS and STATA are fully capable of running cross-tabulations and calculating the associated inferential statistics for between group differences (e.g. *tau b* and *tau c*) and the goodness of fit (χ^2), the full discussion of which goes beyond the scope of this present volume (see Bryman and Cramer 1999; Kulas 2008). It is important to stress, however, that such goodness of fit and association statistics do not prove any kind of causal relationship. Rather, in the example above they merely show that members of particular groups are more or less likely to suffer particular kinds of human rights violations.

For example, in its 2007 report on women's rights and HIV/AIDS in Botswana and Swaziland, Physicians for Human Rights used a survey of 1,268 respondents in Botswana and 788 respondents in Swaziland, who had been randomly chosen and interviewed using primarily closed-ended questions translated into local languages. In addition to showing the different patterns in exposure to HIV/AIDS, positive testing for HIV/AIDS and other descriptive statistics, the report was also able to show evidence of gender discrimination relating to stigmatizing or discriminatory attitudes towards people with HIV, fear about the breakup of their marriages or relationships and fear over the potential to suffer 'intimate partner abuse' upon revelation of their HIV/AIDS status (Physicians for Human Rights 2007: 10). Other findings included issues relating to control over sexual activity, exposure to multiple partners, reasons for unprotected sex and women's lack of autonomy. Table 6.2 provides a good example of how survey-based measures can help analysts arrive at these kinds of conclusions. The table is a summary of results from the Botswana survey carried out by Physicians for Human Rights on reasons why respondents had had unprotected sex. The reasons range from spousal and partner refusals, to ignorance on the use of condoms. The cells report the number and percentage of respondents broken down by gender and list the level of statistical significance. The key statistically significant differences by gender refer to reasons such as a spouse not wanting to have protected sex, a decrease in pleasure, lack of control and inconvenience, while there are no apparent gender differences across the other reasons listed in the survey. This is an example of a cross-tabulation between response categories and gender, which shows the use of multiple questions about the same issue, a breakdown of response by gender and a reporting of statistical significance for gender differences. The larger inferences that are drawn relate to the target population beyond the original sample. In this way, the report is able to link its findings to policy advice on health education in an effort to reduce the prevalence of unprotected sex and the spread of HIV/AIDS. The data show that both of these policy aims must be couched in a larger discourse of gender discrimination and emancipation from patriarchal forms of control, since it is clear in the results that women disproportionately experience pressure from their partners and spouses to have unprotected sex.

Table 6.2 Reasons for unprotected sex in the past 12 months, Botswana community survey

Statement of reason	Men n %	Women n %	Level of significance
Your spouse/partner does not want to	134 (53%)	29 (13%)	0.000
It decreases sexual pleasure	116 (46%)	154 (69%)	0.000
You or your spouse/partner(s) are trying to get pregnant	76 (32%)	78 (32%)	0.248
You use other birth control methods	74 (29%)	80 (36%)	0.130
You have no control over whether your spouse/partner(s) uses a condom	55 (22%)	16 (7%)	0.000
Condoms are inconvenient to use	38 (15%)	65 (29%)	0.000
Condoms do not prevent HIV/AIDS	15 (6%)	11 (5%)	0.635
You cannot afford condoms	13 (5%)	9 (4%)	0.561
Condoms are not available in your area	12 (5%)	13 (6%)	0.610
You do not know how to use a condom	7 (<3%)	6 (<3%)	0.960

Note: Respondents could agree with more than one statement; gender differences in rows 1, 2, 5 and 6 are statistically significant.
Source: Adapted from Physicians for Human Rights (2007: 54).

Limitations to survey-based measures

This chapter has shown the many issues surrounding the use of survey-based measures of human rights. It argued that, like events-based measures and in some way standards-based measures, survey-based measures of human rights rely on a sample of information and then draw inferences about the human rights situation to the whole or target population within a particular context. Unlike events-based and standards-based measures, however, survey-based measures tend to use random samples and avoid many of the problems of inference associated with other methods of human rights measurement. Events-based measures have overcome their inherent biases through the use of multiple sources and, in some ways, those standards-based measures that are transparent about their sources, coding and reliability testing have sought to do the same. However, survey-based measures are in many ways easier to understand, since they collect data from individuals using some form of a structured survey instrument. The responses are then coded and analysed in ways that seek to establish patterns in the perceptions of and experiences with different kinds of human rights. Moreover, survey analysis can then examine the second order relationships between and among different variables linked to the respondents, such as age, gender, income, ethnicity and other categories of social identity and demography. Finally, while survey analysis appears expensive to set up and administer, in relative terms, it can represent a fairly cost-effective way to obtain human rights information.

Despite the many advantages associated with survey-based measures of human rights, there are many pitfalls and limitations to these kinds of data for systematic human rights analysis. Recall that any of the steps involved in the survey process listed in Table 6.1 have the potential to create bias that when carried through the full research process could lead to an over-estimation of human rights problems that may not have occurred, or an underestimation of problems that have occurred. In either case, the security of the inferences that are drawn is fragile and could lead to erroneous policy solutions to particular problems that have seemingly been identified. In particular, any problems with the choice in the design and mode of a survey, the sampling frame, the sampling method and the question wording itself can lead to significant problems in the kinds of conclusions that are drawn from a survey project on human rights. Another problem arises when data collected for one purpose are then used for another purpose; a problem that is not unique to survey-based measures of human rights, but is worth repeating in the context of the discussion here.

Beyond these more general problems, there are additional limitations that need to be noted. First, if a survey project uses a random sample of the whole population, it will uncover fairly low instances in which respondents report that they or someone they know has been a victim of a human rights violation. Such a 'strike rate' will increase if the sample comes from a particularly vulnerable group, but then the first order inferences are limited to that group only. As Physicians for Human Rights have shown, it is possible to combine the results of a survey of an 'at risk' group with social demographic information to arrive at estimations and inferences that extend beyond the original group. Second, reliance on random samples limits the degree to which all individuals are given voice about a human rights situation, which in many ways undermines the fundamental human rights principle of participation and non-discrimination. Reliance on survey instruments alone means that those not selected in the sample are denied the opportunity to tell their stories. Third, random sample surveys provide a limited account of the historical pattern in violations since they tend to be 'snapshots' of the situation rather than retrospective (although in certain instances, such as the surveys in Sierra Leone and East Timor, they were retrospective). Fourth, in contrast to events-based data on human rights, survey data cannot be used to establish lists of victims, perpetrators, or violations. Rather, these data establish patterns in violations expressed in percentage responses to questions that have been formulated *a priori*.

7 Socio-economic and administrative statistics

Introduction

This volume began by suggesting a conceptual model of human rights as derived from international law, which would help clarify the process of monitoring and measurement of human rights. The preceding chapters in the book have looked at various methodological and practical issues concerning measurement and focused on three types of measures that could be used in this exercise – events-based measures, standards-based measures and survey-based measures. A fourth category of measures, i.e. socio-economic and administrative statistics, has also been used to map human rights. Most states collect official statistics on a wide range of issues to determine 'evidence-based policy' and to monitor their performance in the implementation of these policies. The most common data gathering exercise that states undertake is probably the decadal census, which provides updates on demographic indicators like population size, growth, composition and the like. States report on the condition of their economy by collecting information and producing well-recognized indicators/ indices of economic performance like Gross National Product (GNP), per capita income and the production outputs of various sectors of the economy. States with adequate resources also collect baseline information and trends on the execution of various programmes (for example, capacity building of personnel involved in the justice system) and the impact that they have had on the issue concerned (for instance, the prevention, detection and prosecution of crime). While using these data in the measurement of human rights has its advantages, the issue of the validity of these measures has often been raised. When we use these indicators, how do we distinguish between indicators that measure human rights and those that map outcomes of welfare, development and/or governance?

This chapter examines issues related to using socio-economic and administrative statistics (henceforth, official statistics) as human rights indicators. We begin by clarifying the terminology used when referring to these statistics and discuss the questions about measurement validity arising from their application as human rights measures. Three routes have been adopted in the use of official statistics for this purpose: that the indicators cannot be used to measure human rights at all, that the statistics can be used indiscriminately to measure rights, and that the statistics could be used to map some aspects of the concept of human rights. The chapter highlights two approaches that adopt official statistics as valid human rights measures and traces the latest developments in the application of these indicators in human rights monitoring and measurement. The first route adopted is the selection of 'well-being' indicators as justifiable proxies for the measurement of rights, particularly of economic and social rights. The second approach suggests the use of disaggregate measures to map the process of implementing rights obligations of states and highlight *de facto* discrimination, inequality and exclusion. The final section addresses the issue of measurement reliability by addressing the methodological and practical problems associated with the utilization of these indicators and ongoing efforts to tackle these shortcomings.

Official statistics in measurement and monitoring

States routinely produce statistics on a wide range of social and economic issues, which are then used to map baseline performance, set benchmarks of achievement and follow trends in the progress of the implementation of state policies. These statistics may also be used to determine those issue areas that merit state intervention or regulation. Moreover, states routinely monitor current and previous budgetary accounts and expenditure to enable the making and monitoring of evidence-based policy. States also have obligations to collect human rights data and include them in their periodic reports to the various international human rights treaty bodies (see CEDAW 1989; CESCR 1989; CRC 1996; CERD, 2000; CCPR 2001; CAT 2005; CMW 2008). These bodies recommend the use of quantitative measures, including socio-economic and administrative statistics, to monitor states' human rights performance. The mechanisms monitoring the implementation of economic and social rights also require, as a measure of states' obligations to implement economic and social rights to 'the maximum of [their] available resources' (ICESCR Art. 2 (1)), that they report their annual budgetary allocation of and expenditure on the policies initiated towards the provision and protection of these rights (Idasa 2001; Raworth 2001; Norton and Elson 2002; Chapman 2007; Balakrishnan and Elson 2008). Additionally, intergovernmental donor organizations like the World Bank and the International Monetary Fund (IMF), and governmental donors such as the Department for International Development (DFID) in the UK and the Swedish International Development Agency (SIDA), call for states receiving financial assistance from them to set up data collection and management systems to facilitate the assessment of the impact of this assistance on allocated issue areas. For example, one condition placed by the World Bank for receiving development assistance is that states periodically prepare and submit Poverty Reduction Strategy Papers (PRSPs), which should identify key indicators to be used in a baseline assessment of poverty in the country. Governmental donor agencies like DFID and SIDA use these PRSPs, as well as measures of governance and human rights protection, as determinants in their decision to lend financial and technical assistance to these countries (Booth and Lucas 2001; Sida 2003, 2005; Piron and Watkins 2004; Nankani et al. 2005; DFID 2006; Landman 2006b).

These official statistics gathered by states on a broad range of issues have been used as proxies for numerous concepts. Box 7.1 highlights the various ways in which the Human Development Index (HDI), which is a composite indicator of some of these statistics, has been put to use. The indiscriminate and often injudicious use of these measures has resulted in one of the more controversial debates in the measurement of human rights, i.e. the validity of the use of these statistics as measures of or proxies for human rights. According to Adcock and Collier (2001: 531), 'a measurement is valid when scores ... derived from a given indicator ... can meaningfully be interpreted in terms of the systematized concept that the indicator seeks to operationalize'. The question often asked in relation to the validity of official statistics is the extent to which the scores derived from these indicators can be said to reflect the enjoyment of human rights rather than the provision of public goods by the state. This section begins with a brief overview of the terminology that is used when describing these statistics. It also addresses the question of their validity as measures of human rights by highlighting the three arguments suggested in response to the debate on the validity of these measures.

Measures of human rights have included indicators[1] and indices that were originally developed to measure welfare outcomes, human development and governance. However, there is considerable ambiguity in the definitions of these concepts. Although each of these concepts is distinct from the notion of human rights, there may also be areas of overlap (Donnelly 1999; Green 2001; Landman and Häusermann 2003; UNDP 2004, 2006). Welfare could be described as 'all publicly provided and subsidized services, statutory, occupational and fiscal' (Titmuss 1968: 43–44). It has often been measured in terms of the policies implemented and their consequences, e.g. indicators of budgetary allocations and expenditure and the impact this has had on access to food, health and other public provisions (see for example, Cochran and Malone 1995; Clayton and Pontusson 1998; Goodin et al. 2000; Pickvance 2007). The concept of human development was articulated specifically in response to the dependence on economic development as the primary indicator of progress. It was developed to capture the process and outcomes of development and the choices available to people to achieve their goals by 'enhancing their capabilities' (Jahan 2003: 152; see Andreassen 2003; Raworth and Stewart 2003; Sengupta 2003; ul Haq 2003). The most popular measures of this concept are the HDI, which comprises three principal elements captured by four indicators, and the Physical Quality of Life Index (PQLI), which combines three indicators used in the HDI by adopting a simpler statistical method. A detailed discussion of both measures follows below. Governance could be considered to be 'the system of values, policies and institutions' of a society that regulates the relations between the public and private spheres on all issues of importance to the

Box 7.1 Uses and users: For whom and what is the HDI?

Since 1990, academic descriptions of possible uses of the HDI have included: ...

1 challenging GDP as a measure and target of development;
2 helping focus planning objectives;
3 measuring a nation's stock of human wealth;
4 reflecting the impact of policy;
5 analysing alternative development strategies; and
6 directing aid allocations.

How can any single index be expected to perform so many functions: to be both prescriptive and descriptive; a final output and an input; analytical and also an overview; a tool and a target? ... To prevent the HDI becoming a 'Jack of all trades and master of none', an exploration is needed of uses and users of the HDI, so the focus can be on making the HDI a master where it should be.

In the context of the Human Development Reports, the HDI is intended to allow policy-makers to draw a basic picture of their country's level of human development. ... This leads to two fundamental tenets on which the HDI should be based for it to be an effective tool: it is important that the HDI be kept simple for wide comprehension, and that it is based on fundamental dimensions of human development. As such, the interest and usefulness of the HDI to policy-makers would be maximized if the HDI could be:

1 an ideological alternative to GDP;
2 a measure of the stock of human development;
3 a tool for focusing planning objectives (when disaggregated nationally by region/gender/ethnicity); and
4 a reflection of the impact of their policies.

Reproduced from Raworth and Stewart 2003: 164–65

society and polity (UNDP Strategy Note on Governance for Human Development 2004, cited in UNDP 2004: 2). 'Good governance' is an associated concept that equates the impact of governance in a polity with its economic performance. This was later extended by the UNDP to include the political aspects of governance, which has resulted in the development of the concept of 'democratic governance' (Landman and Häusermann 2003; UNDP 2004). A review of the indicators utilized to measure good governance identified five sets of measures, two of which include indicators of civil and political freedoms and the violation of physical integrity rights by the state as proxies for the rule of law and deterioration of good governance (Landman and Häusermann 2003: 28). A human rights indicator, on the other hand, is a measure that maps 'the extent to which a legal right is being fulfilled or enjoyed in a given situation' (Green 2001: 1,065). As discussed previously in this volume, this could include indicators of 'rights-in-principle', 'rights-in-practice' and 'rights-as-policy' (Chapter 2) and a wide range of techniques to develop these indicators (Chapters 4, 5 and 6). Therefore, can measures of welfare, governance, or development be used as valid human rights measures? Are the indicators that measure human rights different in conceptualization or merely in usage from indicators used to map welfare, governance and development?

Three views have been articulated in the literature in answer to this query. The first group of scholars highlights the 'separateness' argument, i.e. the two sets of indicators are different and distinct from each other and cannot be used either interchangeably or as proxy measures for the other. The proposition here is that measures of human rights have little or no overlap with indicators of welfare, governance and development because the indicators measure distinct concepts (see the discussion in Goldstein 1992; Green 2001: 1,090–91; and Raworth 2001). If we accept this approach, development, governance and welfare indicators could still be utilized in parallel with human rights indicators to examine the conditions that favour or deter the protection of human rights. For example, some of the debates echoed in the literature on public health, medicine and the right to health outline the 'reciprocal impact of health and human rights'. This view recognizes that governmental policies and practices on health have an indelible impact on a range of human rights (and not just on the right to health) and that the protection (or violation) of these rights affects the health and well-being of individuals (Mann et al. 1999; Gruskin and Tarantola 2005).

The second approach in this debate is the 'sameness' argument, which holds that human rights indicators and development statistics map concepts that have considerable overlap and can, therefore, be used interchangeably. It has been argued that human development is a culmination of and includes the enjoyment of human rights, including civil and political rights. Although individuals have responsibility for their basic needs, states are obligated to ensure that individuals are not unjustifiably hindered in the pursuit of these goals and are provided with at least the minimum resources and services towards this end (Eide summarized in Andreassen 2003: 218–21). This approach would argue that the enjoyment of the outcomes of development and rights would be identical. Hence, the indicators used to measure these concepts would also be the same (see for example, indicators used by the United Nations Children's Fund (UNICEF) in its annual reports on the *State of the World's Children*, by the United Nations Educational, Scientific and Cultural Organization (UNESCO) in its annual *Global Education Digest*, and by United Nations Development Fund for Women's (UNIFEM) annual publication on the *Progress of the World's Women*).

The third approach that has been suggested to address the issue of validity of human rights measures is the 'proxy' argument. If we accept that the concepts of human rights, development, governance and welfare overlap, then statistics measuring the latter could be used to measure some elements of human rights. Thus, while the difference between the various sets of indicators is acknowledged, it is equally accepted that these indicators can be used to measure certain aspects of the obligations of states to implement human rights (see Mann et al. 1999; Hunt et al. 2002; Gruskin et al. 2005 and Backman et al. 2008 for applications of this position to health; also see Green 2001; Landman and Häusermann 2003; Sengupta 2003; Landman 2006b; Chapman 2007). The UNDP *Human Development Report 2000* elaborates on the similarities and differences between the two types of indicators. Both sets of indicators have in common a) the goal to realize human freedoms, b) reliance on inputs and outcomes as measures, and c) the use of disaggregated data, averages, and global and local data. What is distinct about the indicators is a) their conceptual foundations, b) their focus of attention where development indicators address human inputs and outcomes while human rights indicators also tackle policies and practices, and c) additional information that human rights indicators require, for example on violations of rights as well as processes, institutions and frameworks compared to development indicators (UNDP 2000: 91). A similar distinction has been reiterated between indicators of children's rights and those of child well-being (Ennew 1997; Boyce 2005).

Using official statistics to measure human rights

Given these three perspectives on the validity of officially collected statistics as indicators of human rights, advocates of using such indicators have taken two routes to develop and use official statistics as valid and reliable human rights measures: the use of aggregate statistics like the HDI and PQLI as proxies for measuring rights in practice, and the use of disaggregate statistics as measures of rights in policy and non-discrimination in practice.

Aggregate statistics: measuring rights in practice

The use of the HDI and the PQLI as proxy measures for the enjoyment of economic and social rights is probably a reflection of the 'basic rights' argument elaborated in Chapter 2. The claim made here is that the indicators included within these indices represent the enjoyment of rights that are the cornerstone for the protection of other rights recognized in international human rights law. The identification of a key set of indicators to measure human rights makes it easier for states to collect data, place a significantly lesser burden on state resources, and may be valuable in providing a glimpse into the protection and provision of these rights (also see Raworth 2001; Mokhiber 2005; Apodaca 2007). The HDI was developed to address the dissatisfaction with Gross Domestic Product (GDP) as a measure of 'human welfare', as opposed to an indicator of economic development. The authors of the measure wanted to develop an indicator that would capture the essential elements of the term 'human development' and produce a standard to assess the progress of states. This measure would address not just the economic aspects of development, but the increase in individual capabilities required to pursue this development. The HDI is a scale from 0 to 1 that captures the average level of attainments in longevity, knowledge and income. These are measured by four indicators: life expectancy, literacy rate, gross enrolment ratio and per capita GDP, which are assigned special weights during the calculation of the score (Anand and Sen 2003; Jahan 2003; ul Haq 2003).

The HDI has been used as a direct measure of the achievement of states in these key areas (see Figure 7.1). In this mould, the HDI score is a simple representation of the basic minimum welfare provisions that a state has made available to its population. If the score a country receives is closer to 1 on the HDI scale, this can be interpreted as the state's relatively good performance in the aim to provide its population with the basic capabilities to engage in the fullest pursuit of their goals. The HDI can also be used for policy analysis by highlighting differences in the achievements on the indicators included in the index on the grounds of class, gender, ethnic group, geographical region, administrative unit, etc. For example, in Figure 7.2 (reproduced from the UNDP's *Human Development Report 2000*), the national average of the HDI for Nepal masks the differences in the achievements enjoyed by various ethnic groups within Nepali society. Thus, while members of the Newar and Brahmin communities in the state enjoy an HDI of 0.450, members of the Muslim community are at the level of 0.240. A caveat on the interpretation of the HDI scores is that the increase or decrease of a country's HDI score over time should not be interpreted as a direct result of the implementation of state policies in these three areas, as two of the four indicators (life expectancy and adult literacy) used in the construction of the HDI change incrementally over time (Anand and Sen 2003; Andreassen 2003; Fukuda-Parr et al. 2003; Jahan 2003; Landman 2006a). The HDI has also been used as a proxy for economic and social rights in research since it captures the enjoyment of two basic rights – education and health – as mediated by individual economic capacity (Moon and Dixon 1985, 1992; Kimenyi 2007). The authors of the HDI accept that the index does not measure all aspects of human development. However, they also maintain that by limiting the number of variables included in the index to a theoretically justified set of basic features necessary for the development of individual capabilities, they are able to reduce the complexity in measurement while ensuring cost-effectiveness in the collection of data and the use of easily available indicators (Andreassen 2003; Fukuda-Parr et al. 2003; Jahan 2003; ul Haq 2003).

In addition to the HDI, the UNDP has also developed the Gender-related Development Index (GDI) and a Gender Empowerment Index (GEM). The GDI is the HDI measure adjusted for inequalities based on gender. It includes the same indicators as the HDI – life expectancy, literacy rate, gross enrolment ratio and per capita GDP; however, this measure takes into consideration the differences between men and women in the enjoyment of these variables. The

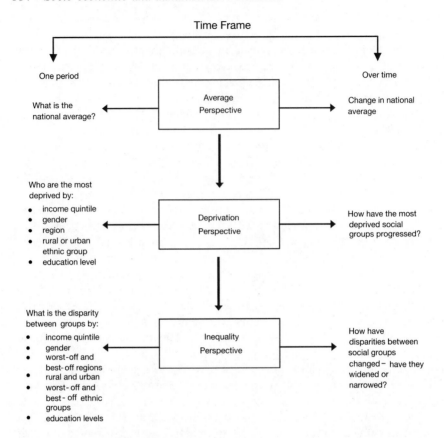

Figure 7.1 Three perspectives for assessing progress using the Human Development
　　　　　Index
Source: Fukuda-Parr et al. 2003: 181

GEM measures the extent of participation of women in the polity and the
economy, and their influence on and input into decision-making. Like the
disaggregate HDI measures, the GEM is a tool that can be used to unravel
the gender disparities in society and the polity. It can assist policy-makers and
advocacy groups to promote targeted policies aimed at reducing these differences in general attainments (technical note in UNDP 2000; Jahan 2003;
UNDP 2004: 44–45).

The PQLI is another aggregate measure that has been widely utilized to map
the enjoyment of subsistence or economic and social rights. Like the HDI,
which was developed in the 1990s, the PQLI was created by Morris David
Morris in 1979 to counter the excessive dependence of the academic and
policy community on GNP and other indicators of economic development as
measures of the overall progress of states. The PQLI is a scale that runs from

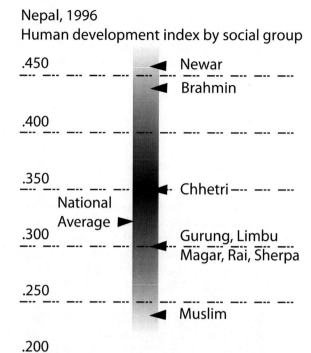

Nepal, 1996
Human development index by social group

Figure 7.2 Disaggregating the average can reveal discrimination
Source: UNDP. 2000: 97

0 to 100 and comprises the arithmetic mean of equally weighted indicators of infant mortality, life expectancy and adult literacy. These indicators have been chosen to capture the direct and indirect effects of public health, nutrition and social relations, and the potential for development. Each indicator measures the actual enjoyment of basic rights to health and education and not the potential that states possess to provide for these rights (which the GNP measure would signify). Thus, this measure seeks to capture government *outcomes* rather than government *effort*. A higher score on the scale indicates that the state in question is able to provide its citizens with basic minimum enjoyment of economic and social rights in a particular year (Moon and Dixon 1985, 1992; Hofferbert and Cingranelli 1996; Callaway and Harrelson-Stephens 2004; Milner et al. 2004; Landman 2006b; Cingranelli and Richards 2007).

The PQLI has been criticized on two grounds: the construction of the index and its utilization in academic and policy research. The equal weighting scheme adopted to create the index has been faulted on the grounds that no theoretical justification has been provided for this approach. Consequently, some authors have suggested that each of the three components be assigned different weights depending on the relative importance and linkages between the elements. Further, the PQLI has been used as a measure of the enjoyment of subsistence rights as well as the provision of welfare. What it is unable to capture is the *process* aspect of the concept of human rights or government effort in implementing these rights (see discussion in subsequent section). It also fails to map differences in distribution of the public provisions within developed countries. Moreover, it has been noted that an aggregated measure would be unable to distinguish between the interactions and trade-offs between the measures used in the composite measure (Goldstein 1992; Milner et al. 2004; Apodaca 2007: 177–78).

Disaggregate statistics: measuring rights in policy and practice

In response to criticisms about the construction and utilization of the aggregate measures mentioned above, it has been suggested that individual measures be selected (based on appropriate and accepted theoretical justifications and data availability) to measure the outcomes of the enjoyment of human rights (Donnelly and Howard 1988; Apodaca 2007). Thus, the individual elements of the two aggregate measures discussed above have been used as distinct measures of human rights. Infant mortality rate per 10,000 births, life expectancy at age one, percentage of adult literacy and gross enrolment ratio have been utilized as proxy measures of the right to health, the right to life and the right to education, respectively. These indices primarily measure the outcomes of the *obligations of result* (rights in practice) of the state. However, official statistics could also be utilized as measures or proxies of the *obligations of conduct* (rights as policy). This partially reflects what has been referred to as an 'information pyramid', which consists of key measures of the right, indicators that measure the implementation of the programme for the provision of the right, and the socio-economic context within which the implementation takes place (Kempf in Apodaca 2007: 175–77). It also coincides with structural, process and outcome indicators identified by Paul Hunt in his reports on the right to health to the United Nations General Assembly and Commission on Human Rights (Hunt 2003a, 2004a, and 2006; UN 2006, 2008).

Official statistics have been often used as measures of the actual enjoyment of rights. Long-term outcomes of state policies providing for public goods and services have been treated as proxies for the protection of a range of human rights. When these statistics are disaggregated on grounds of gender, region, religion, ethnicity and other factors that may attract inequalities and marginalization, they assist policy makers and advocates in mapping the outcomes of the enjoyment of rights and highlighting *de facto* discrimination and exclusion (Hunt et al. 2002; Apodaca 2007; de Beco 2007). International, regional and national agencies collect, collate and reproduce these statistics in annual reports on the enjoyment of rights by a particular vulnerable group, like women, children, or refugees (see, for example, UNIFEM 2005; UNHCR 2006; UNICEF 2009) or the protection and provision of key subsistence rights such as health, food and education (for example, FAO 2008; UNESCO 2009; WHO 2008).

The collection of statistics on civil and political rights, however, is biased towards rights in practice or outcome indicators as compared to indicators collected on economic, social and cultural rights. Official statistics such as crime records and election statistics are easily found across states and utilized as measures of the protection of civil and political rights, including personal integrity rights. However, the enjoyment of economic, social and cultural rights is also a result of the actions of state and non-state actors and, hence, these indicators would need to measure the specific impact of these distinct actors. Human development, governance, or welfare indicators that are used as proxies for the measurement of economic, social and cultural rights and official statistics used to measure civil and political rights often do not incorporate this distinction (Cingranelli and Richards 2007).

In addition to being adopted as measures of the 'results' of the enjoyment of rights, official statistics have also been utilized to assess state policies that have been implemented to give effect to certain rights. This has been termed as measuring *government effort* to provide for the minimal protections and provisions, as opposed to measuring the outcomes of these efforts. The impetus towards developing and using such measures arises from states' legal obligations of *conduct* with respect to implementing human rights in addition to their obligations of *result*. This is especially reflected with respect to economic, social and cultural rights towards which each state is required to

> take steps, individually and through international assistance and co-operation, especially economic and technical, to the maximum of its available resources, with a view to achieving progressively the full realization of the rights recognized in the present Covenant by all appropriate means, including particularly the adoption of legislative measures
> (Art. 2 (1) of the *International Covenant on Economic, Social and Cultural Rights*).

These *process* indicators attempt to track the initiation, implementation and outcomes of specific policies and programmes that states enact to uphold their international human rights obligations. Process indicators comprise financial inputs and the resulting goods, facilities and personnel needed for the protection and provision of rights. Table 7.1 suggests potential structural, process and outcome indicators that could be developed or collected to measure state obligations towards the right to food. The logic behind the development and use of these indicators is the cause-and-effect relationship between the three levels of indicators (as elaborated in Chapter 2). Structural indicators map the international and domestic legal commitments of states. It is based on these commitments that states can be held to account for the policies and programmes they implemented and which can be measured using process indicators. Outcome indicators map the 'results' of state efforts. These statistics allow for an in-depth assessment of the implementation of a state's obligations by taking into account not just the outcomes (which may be affected

by the positive actions of non-state actors) but the measures adopted specifically by states towards the fulfilment of these obligations (Hunt et al. 2002;
Hunt 2003a, 2004a, and 2006; Landman and Häusermann 2003; Asher 2004;
Künnemann and Epal-Ratjen 2004; Rosenblum 2004; Landman 2006a; UN
2006, 2008; Apodaca 2007; Chapman 2007).

Monitoring the implementation of human rights by states can also be carried out by assessing where and how states spend their money. An audit of a
state's fiscal and monetary policies, income, taxation and expenditure using
human rights principles in conjunction with its legal human rights obligations
is one way of assessing the extent to which states abide by their obligation to
utilize the maximum available resources towards the progressive and full realization of rights, especially economic, social and cultural rights (see Box 7.2).
It has been proposed that such an audit should be based on the following
principles: progressive realization and non-retrogression, maximum available
resources, non-discrimination and equality, minimum core obligations, and
transparency, accountability and participation. The state is endowed with
obligations of conduct and obligations of result when incorporating these
principles in its economic policies, which should also be assessed during this
exercise (Balakrishnan and Elson 2008; Balakrishnan et al. 2009). State budgets are useful tools to conduct such an audit of state policies. Budgets are
official statements on the policies implemented in the previous fiscal year, the
programmes planned for the coming year and the financial capacity of the
state to carry out its plans. They enable human rights advocates, researchers,
civil society organizations, communities and individuals to assess the extent to
which states convert their legal obligations towards human rights into policy
commitments by mapping the resource share allocated to these programmes.
Budgets also help determine annual governmental priorities in spending and
taxation. They could be utilized to assess the impact that certain policies may
have on the enjoyment of a range of rights and on vulnerable groups (Idasa
2001; Norton and Elson 2002; Fundar et al. 2004; Chapman 2007).

It has been noted, however, that monitoring of the process of implementation is often restricted to economic, social and cultural rights. It was long
assumed that civil and political rights primarily create negative obligations on
the state, which are of immediate effect. However, the obligations of states to
protect and provide these rights include financial investments in training of
law enforcement and judicial personnel in human rights principles and standards, law enforcement and judicial infrastructure, the time taken to process
judicial cases, etc. (Hofferbert and Cingranelli 1996; Landman and Häusermann 2003; Cingranelli and Richards 2007; Balakrishnan and Elson
2008). Recent intergovernmental and national efforts have sought to clarify
the nature of monitoring state obligations towards civil and political rights.
The United States Agency for International Development (USAID 1998)
developed a handbook of indicators to assist its staff in aid-recipient states in
monitoring the implementation and enjoyment of these rights. However, the
handbook does not provide data on these indicators; rather it is a guide

Table 7.1 List of illustrative indicators on the right to adequate food (UDHR, Art. 25) (* MDG related indicators)

	Nutrition	Food safety and consumer protection	Food availability	Food accessibility
Structural	International human rights treaties, relevant to the right to adequate food, ratified by the State • Date of entry into force and coverage of the right to adequate food in the Constitution or other forms of superior law • Date of entry into force and coverage of domestic laws for implementing the right to adequate food • Number of registered and/or active non-governmental organizations (per 100,000 persons) involved in the promotion and protection of the right to adequate food			
	• Time frame and coverage of national policy on nutrition and nutrition adequacy norms	• Time frame and coverage of national policy on food safety and consumer protection • Number of registered and/or active civil society organisations working in the area of food safety and consumer protection	• Time frame and coverage of national policy on agricultural production and food availability • Time frame and coverage of national policy on drought, crop failure and disaster management	
Process	• Proportion of received complaints on the right to adequate food investigated and adjudicated by the national human rights institution, human rights ombudsperson or other mechanism and the proportion of these responded to effectively by the government • Net official development assistance (ODA) for food security received or provided as a proportion of public expenditure on food security or Gross National Income			
	• Proportion of targeted population that was brought above the minimum level of dietary energy consumption* in the reporting period • Proportion of targeted population covered under public nutrition supplement programmes	• Disposal rate or average time to adjudicate a case registered in a consumer court • Share of public social sector budget spent on food safety and consumer protection advocacy, education, research and implementation of law and regulations relevant to the right	• Proportion of female headed households or targeted population with legal title to agricultural land • Arable irrigated land per person • Proportion of farmers availing extension services	• Share of household consumption of major food items for targeted population group met through publicly assisted programmes • Unemployment rate or average wage rate of targeted segments of labour force • Proportion of targeted population that was brought above the poverty line in the reporting period

Table 7.1 (continued)

	Nutrition	Food safety and consumer protection	Food availability	Food accessibility
	• Coverage of targeted population under public programmes on nutrition education and awareness • Proportion of targeted population that was extended access to an improved drinking water source* in the reporting period	• Proportion of food producing and distributing establishments inspected for food quality standards and frequency of inspections • Proportion of cases adjudicated under food safety and consumer protection law in the reporting period	• Share of public budget spent on strengthening domestic agricultural production (e.g. agriculture-extension, irrigation, credit, marketing) • Proportion of per capita availability of major food items sourced through domestic production, import & amp; food-aid • Cereal import dependency ratio in the reporting period	• Work participation rates, by sex and target groups • Estimated access of women and girls to adequate food within household • Coverage of programmes to secure access to productive resources for target groups
Outcome	• Prevalence of underweight and stunting children under-five years of age* • Proportion of adults with body-mass index (BMI) <18.5	• Number of recorded deaths and incidence of food poisoning related to adulterated food	• Per capita availability of major food items of local consumption	• Proportion of population below minimum level of dietary energy consumption*/ proportion of undernourished population • Average household expenditure on food for the bottom three deciles of population or targeted population
	• Death rates, including infant and under-five mortality rates, associated with and prevalence of malnutrition (including under-, over-nutrition and inadequate intake of nutrients)			
24.4.08	*All indicators* should be disaggregated by prohibited grounds of discrimination, as applicable and reflected in metasheets			

Source: UN 2008: 24.

Box 7.2 Conducting a human rights audit of economic policy in a country, in relation to economic and social rights

In conducting an audit, we suggest the following stages:

1 select the economic policies to be considered;
2 identify which of the [human rights] principles apply most directly to the selected policies;
3 identify relevant indicators to assess how far obligations of conduct are being met;
4 identify indicators of results in realizing economic and social rights, and use them to cross check indicators of conduct where appropriate…

We draw a distinction between an audit and a study of policy impact. The latter purports to establish a causal link between economic policies and the degree of substantive enjoyment of economic and social rights ('results'). … An audit has a less ambitious aim: to examine how policy has been conducted – whether it has consisted of action 'reasonably calculated to realize the enjoyment of a particular right'. …

Where appropriate, the analysis of conduct can be cross-checked with a quantitative and qualitative analysis of relevant 'results' for some relevant rights. The data on 'results' may reinforce or challenge the conclusions about the conduct of policy. For example, in considering public expenditure, we may examine whether public expenditure on health might be considered to be 'action reasonably calculated to realize' the right to health in a way that complies with obligations for non-discrimination and equality. If we find that public expenditure is very unequally distributed between different social groups, this suggests a *prima facie* case of failure to meet obligation of conduct. We can cross-check this with data on the health status of different social groups (which measure some dimension of how far they enjoy particular levels of the right to health). If we find the health status of the group with the lowest share of expenditure is worse than those groups with higher shares of expenditure, this suggests that the government is indeed in violation of its obligations of conduct. …

None of this implies that health expenditure is the only form of public expenditure that has an impact on the right to health, or that public expenditure is the only economic policy instrument that has an impact on the right to health. The enjoyment of the right to health is the outcome of numerous factors, and the audit does not seek to establish what those factors are. It has the more modest goal of investigating whether policy on public expenditure appears to be in compliance with obligations on the right to health.

Reproduced from Balakrishnan and Elson 2008: 8–9

suggesting the need for further progress in the process of monitoring by adopting these indicators. Various UN agencies, in particular the Office of the High Commissioner for Human Rights (OHCHR), have also contributed immensely to advancing the efforts in the measurement of the process of implementing civil and political rights. The levels of structure, process and outcome indicators have been successfully applied to mapping a number of civil and political rights (UN 2006, 2008). In Table 7.2, this framework has been applied to the right to liberty and security of the person. The indicators highlighted in the framework for each right have been derived from the interpretation of the nature of state obligations in international human rights law towards the right. However, this leads to the identification of processes and actions that may be difficult to quantify or measure. For example, data for the indicators measuring the violations of due process to those persons being legally detained without recourse to judicial or other oversight, or on the proportion or number of arrests made under a state's lawful administrative detention provisions would be difficult to obtain. Although these indicators, if collected, would be valid measures, it is highly unlikely that most states would be able to devote financial resources and personnel to monitoring these aspects of the implementation of their rights obligations, or be willing to share this data on the grounds of national security or public interest.

Assessing the use of official statistics

The final section of this chapter addresses the shortcomings in using official statistics as measures of human rights. It touches upon methodological issues and practical problems in human rights measurement using these indicators. The section also highlights the issue of state capacity in building and maintaining data management systems and refers to efforts by intergovernmental and non-governmental organizations to assist states in this endeavour.

Since socio-economic and administrative statistics are collected by states, the obvious question that is raised at the outset is how much we can trust that these data are a faithful representation of reality. States reporting on their human rights obligations might have an incentive to manipulate official statistics and present an unduly favourable depiction of their human rights record. A recent study has shown that data collection also presents an opportunity for governments to perpetuate human rights abuses. Seltzer and Anderson (2008) have found that vulnerable groups such as members of ethnic, religious, or linguistic minorities, indigenous populations and subject populations have been targeted by the state during the process of administering the periodic population census in the territory, or the implementation of some other form of population registration system. Records show that these groups were systematically subjected to forced migration, internment, voter disenfranchisement, ethnic cleansing or genocide.

States that do not choose this insidious route to statistical reporting might still produce human rights statistics that are under-reported or depend on

Table 7.2 List of Illustrative indicators on the right to liberty and security of person (UDHR, Art. 3)

	Arrest and detention based on criminal charges	Administrative deprivation of liberty	Effective review by court	Security from crime and abuse by law enforcement officials
Structural	• International human rights treaties, relevant to the right to liberty and security of person, ratified by the State • Date of entry into force and coverage of the right to liberty and security of person in the Constitution or other forms of superior law • Date of entry into force and coverage of domestic laws for implementing the right to liberty and security of person • Time frame and coverage of policy and administrative framework against any arbitrary deprivations of liberty, whether based on criminal charges, sentences or decisions by a court or administrative framework against any arbitrary deprivations of liberty, whether based on criminal charges, sentences or decisions by a court or administrative grounds (e.g. immigration, mental illness, educational purposes, vagrancy) • Type of accreditation of National Human Rights Institutions by the rules of procedure of the International Coordinating Committee of National Institutions		• Legal time limits for an arrested or detained person before being informed of the reasons for the arrest or detention; before being brought to or having the case reviewed by an authority exercising judicial power; and for the trial duration of a person in detention	• Time frame and coverage of policy and administrative framework on security, handling of criminality and abuses by law enforcement officials
Process	• Proportion of received complaints on the right to liberty and security of person investigated and adjudicated by the national human rights institution, human rights ombudsperson or other mechanisms and the proportion of these responded to effectively by the government • Proportion of communications sent by the UN Working Group on Arbitrary Detention responded to effectively by the government • Proportion of law enforcement officials (including police, military and State security force) trained in rules of conduct concerning the proportional use of force, arrest, detention, interrogation or punishment	• Number/proportion of arrests or entries into detention under national administrative provisions (e.g. security, immigration control, mental illness and other medical grounds, educational purposes, drug addiction, financial obligations) in the reporting period • Number/proportion of releases from administrative detentions in the reporting period	• Proportion of cases where the time for arrested or detained persons before being informed of the reasons of arrest; before receiving notice of the charge (in legal sense); or before being informed of the reasons of administrative detention exceeded the respective legally stipulated time limit	• Proportion of law enforcement officials formally investigated for physical and non-physical abuse or crime, including arbitrary arrest and detention (based on criminal or administrative grounds) in the reporting period • Proportion of formal investigations of law enforcement officials resulting in disciplinary actions or prosecution in the reporting period
	• Number/proportion of arrests or entries into detention (pre- and pending trial) on the basis of a court order or due to action taken directly by executive authorities in the reporting period • Number/proportion of defendants released from pre- and trial detentions in exchange for bail or due to non-filing of charges in the reporting period			

Table 7.2 (continued)

Arrest and detention based on criminal charges	Administrative deprivation of liberty	Effective review by court	Security from crime and abuse by law enforcement officials
		• Number of *habeas corpus* and similar petitions filed in courts in the reporting period • Proportion of arrested or detained persons provided with access to a counsellor or legal aid • Proportion of cases subject to review by a higher court or appellate body • Reported cases where pre- and trial detentions exceeded the legally stipulated time limit in the reporting period	• Number of persons arrested, adjudicated, convicted or serving sentence for violent crime (including homicide, rape, assault) per 100,000 population in the reporting period • Proportion of law enforcement officials killed in line of duty in the reporting period • Firearms owners per 100,000 population/Number of firearms licences withdrawn in the reporting period • Proportion of violent crimes with the use of firearms • Proportion of violent crimes reported to the police (victimisation survey) in the reporting period
Outcome • Number of detentions per 100,000 population, on the basis of a court order or due action by executive authorities at the end of the reporting period • Reported cases of arbitrary detentions, including post-trial detentions (e.g. as reported to the UN Working Group on Arbitrary Detention) in the reporting period		• Proportion of arrests and detentions declared unlawful by national courts • Proportion of victims released and compensated after arrests or detentions declared unlawful by judicial authority	• Proportion of population feeling 'unsafe', (e.g. walking alone in area after dark or alone at home at night) • Incidence and prevalence of physical and non-physical abuse or crime, including by law enforcement officials in line of duty, per 100,000 population, in the reporting period
All indicators should be disaggregated by prohibited grounds of discrimination, as applicable and reflected in metasheets			

24.04.08

Source: UN 2008: 23.

unreliable primary sources of information. For example, relying on police records of arbitrary detention as the sole source of information on torture, extrajudicial killings and forced disappearances might lead to grossly under-reported statistics. Moreover, cross-country comparisons using these statistics are not always valid, because different countries use different definitions and classifications in their data collection and apply a range of methods to collect the data (Goldstein 1992; Samuelson and Spirer 1992; Freedman 1999; Raworth 2001; Landman and Häusermann 2003; Apodaca 2007). However, despite these drawbacks, the most important advantage of using official statistics is that states accept these as undisputed facts and agree to be held accountable for them. Basic administrative and official statistics like the population census, registries of births and deaths, property regulation, etc., can be used to highlight sudden shocks or trends in the data, which might signal gross human rights abuses (Landman 2006a; Spirer and Seltzer 2008).

As discussed above, there is widespread agreement among different sections of the human rights community that the development of indicators is primarily an obligation of the state. However, data collection and management is a serious challenge faced by many countries, which lack the infrastructure and capacity for collecting such data and making them accessible. International intergovernmental organizations have recognized the importance of assisting states in the development of indicators and the creation and maintenance of data collection systems. The World Health Organization (WHO), UNICEF, Food and Agriculture Organization (FAO), UNESCO and the International Labour Organization (ILO) have all undertaken programmes or enacted policies towards capacity building of states in meeting this obligation (ILO 2006; de Beco 2007; WHO 2008; UNESCO 2009; UNICEF 2009). The UNDP and the OHCHR (UNDP 1998) began a 'Programme for Human Rights Strengthening', which consisted of assisting states to develop capacity towards human rights protection. This involved helping states draft comprehensive national plans towards implementing their human rights obligations, building and maintaining data collection, management and dissemination systems, and documenting good practice in their efforts to provide such technical assistance. Since then, these UN agencies have been successful in further clarifying the content of human rights monitoring and measurement, especially in relation to civil and political rights (RMAP 2004; Mokhiber 2005; UN 2006, 2008)

International and national donor organizations and non-governmental organizations have also begun working in tandem with states to build domestic capacity and infrastructure in data management. The Comprehensive Development Framework (CDF) was a set of principles proposed by the World Bank in 1999 for states to adopt as a policy framework for poverty reduction and sustainable development. The PRSPs, which are built upon the CDF principles, were adopted by the World Bank and the IMF as the set of guidelines and processes that would determine debt relief to Heavily Indebted Poor Countries (HIPC). One of the five core principles on which the PRSPs are based involves assisting states in developing data collection and management systems and capacity building, to analyse and disseminate these data.

The process of drafting the PRSPs and their outcomes have been assessed for the extent to which they adhere to human rights-based approach by incorporating the principles of participation, accountability, transparency, equitability and non-discrimination (Claude and Jabine 1992; Booth and Lucas 2001; Sengupta 2003; Nankani et al. 2005). The Organisation for Economic Co-operation and Development (OECD) Metagora project, which commenced in 2004, was initiated to develop 'methods, tools, and frameworks for enhancing evidence-based assessment of democracy, human rights, and governance'. Additionally, various pilot programmes and three ongoing projects were started to contribute to filling the capacity gap between developed and developing countries for data collection and analysis (Suesser and Suarez de Miguel 2008).

Summary

All states collect some form of administrative data for a variety of purposes. The trend in 'evidence-based policy-making', monitoring of international commitments to human development, and state obligations to report on the implementation of human rights has led to a marked increase in the depth and breadth of official statistics being produced by states. These statistics are often readily available and accessible and, therefore, end up being the first point of reference when individuals and groups commence human rights monitoring and measurement. Given that these statistics have been produced by states, they possess tremendous influence as an officially accepted depiction of the condition of rights enjoyment in a country at a particular time. It is important that such data be used judiciously, with a clear understanding of what is being measured (to ensure measurement validity), and the limitations and strengths of its use (to retain measurement reliability).

8   Conclusion

It is clear from this volume that the measurement of human rights is a thriving and burgeoning field involving scholars and practitioners from academic institutions across the disciplines of political science, sociology, economics and statistics; international and domestic non-governmental organizations; intergovernmental organizations such as the World Bank, the United Nations and the European Commission; and governments themselves, either as donors or as recipient countries engaged in state party reporting on human rights, drafting and implementing Poverty Reduction Strategy Papers (PRSPs), or governance assessments and human rights analysis. The chapters presented here have tried to outline, synthesize and evaluate the existing efforts at measuring human rights, in a way that is grounded in a set of assumptions that recognize the importance of the international law of human rights and the many ways in which the implementation of human rights varies across the many different cultural contexts of the world. The core chapters on existing human rights measures, in their own way, have shown that there is now a large body of work that uses the standard tools of the social sciences and statistics to provide valid, reliable and meaningful measures of human rights.

However, it is also clear from this volume that as the sources and levels of information have become more robust, the human rights community needs to continue to improve the degree to which it monitors, measures and analyses human rights. Indeed, we believe that there are a series of conceptual, methodological and policy lessons that emerge from this book that, when heeded, can help improve and strengthen existing efforts at measurement and lead to new initiatives that are more sensitive to the issues of measurement addressed here. We have shown that we now know more about *what* to measure conceptually and legally, than *how* to measure it. We also know that a large part of this human rights content remains *unmeasured,* and that those parts that are measured tend to rely too much on particular types of measures, which have a number of significant limitations that affect their validity, reliability and substantive meaning. In this way, the measurement project is incomplete and significant gaps exist and challenges remain for this exciting area of work. It is to these remaining issues that this final chapter addresses itself, arguing that policy analysis and implementation, human rights scholarship, and advocacy at the domestic and international level must rest on the highest quality of systematic evidence available.

Conceptual lessons

Chapter 2 showed that there has been tremendous development in our understanding of the core content of human rights, which has moved on considerably since the idea of *international human* rights was formally articulated in the 1948 *Universal Declaration of Human Rights* and the subsequent international and regional instruments. This content has emerged through long and contested processes of consultation, adjudication and deliberation, in ways that have helped provide the *systematized concepts* necessary for the operationalization of human rights into indicators and eventually scores on units. The debates about human rights have moved beyond the simple distinction between and among the 'generations' of rights, the arguments that some rights are more important than others, and the idea that some rights are negative and some rights are positive. Rather, the thinking on human rights sees them much more holistically, where all rights are afforded equal status, that they are separate but often inter-related in complex ways, and that states have the legal obligation to respect, protect and fulfil all human rights. This final development has meant that the measurement effort has much work to do in finding solutions for measuring these three different state obligations. To date, existing measures are biased towards the measurement of civil and political rights, and the measures for these rights are biased towards the state obligation to respect, effectively ignoring the obligation to protect (i.e. from third-party violations) and to fulfil (i.e. state provision of resources into progressive realization). Those measures that have been developed for economic and social rights have tended to focus on the obligation to fulfil and have, therefore, ignored the obligations to respect and protect. Further conceptual work thus needs to be done on these underdeveloped dimensions of human rights in ways that will help devise measures for them.

Methodological lessons

All measurement involves the translation of an abstract concept into some kind of quantified expression that is valid, reliable and meaningful, while the act of measurement involves the use of some kind of sample of information that serves as the basis for the moment of quantification. The key lesson from this volume is that the experience of human rights as an *empirical record* is highly biased, incomplete and prone to significant error in any attempt to measure it. The two fundamental errors include the *under-reporting* of rights violations that have occurred, or the *over-reporting* of violations that have not. Any measurement effort thus needs to find ways to contend with the causes of error, including the selection of sources, the number of sources, the development of a coding scheme, the use of that scheme, the testing of the reliability of the scheme, and the use of appropriate statistical methods for analysing the measures once they have been produced. We saw that in the case of some of the standards-based measures, source material is unknown or unreported; the coding scheme is less than transparent; tests on the reliability of the coding have not been done; and the scales themselves have the particular problem of variance truncation, where complex and highly variable information on human rights practices across different countries is reduced down to a handful of discrete coding categories.

Since the original political terror scale at Purdue University and the freedom scales were devised by Raymond D. Gastil, however, efforts have been made to address some of these more egregious methodological problems. For example, the Cingranelli and Richards human rights data project has been transparent about its source material, coding procedures and use of inter-rater reliability tests. The sources are referenced, the code book clearly spells out the threshold conditions for the categories in each scale and the use of multiple coding teams to enhance the degree of reliability is explained. The political terror scale in its current manifestation is much more attentive to its coding procedure and reliability testing, while the academic team at the University of North Carolina Asheville is developing a broader range of scores beyond the standard 1 to 5 to alleviate the worst forms of variance truncation. Future work on standards-based measures should draw on these lessons to avoid the worst forms of bias, in order to provide the best measures for cross-national time-series analysis.

Work in the field of events-based measures has advanced tremendously since the early days of newspaper coding. The work of the American Association for the Advancement of Science (in particular Herbert Spirer, Patrick Ball and Audrey Chapman) and now Benetech has focused on source materials, validity and reliability. As a consequence, the use of multiple systems estimation (MSE) has allowed for the generation of highly valid and reliable event counting for particular periods of history in particular cultural contexts. This work has, in many ways, approached a 'normal science' (see Kuhn 1962) of human rights events-coding and statistical analysis. In deconstructing the *grammar* of human rights events, the 'who did what to whom' model has provided the most micro-measures of human rights events, where the violation itself has become the basic unit of analysis. The attention of this work, though, like that of the political terror scale, has tended to be on a very discrete set of violations relating to personal integrity rights. The challenge for this type of measure is to broaden the horizon of rights beyond extra-judicial killings, disappearances, detention, torture and rape, to include violations such as electoral intimidation, social and economic discrimination, and healthcare discrimination, among many others.

Survey-based measures for human rights are relatively new and, like standards-based and events-based measures, involve a series of trade-offs. On the one hand, the use of random samples of a large number of respondents allows for strong inferences to be drawn and the use of closed-survey instruments means that a research team can collect and analyse data relatively quickly since the response categories are predetermined. On the other hand, mass random samples tend to uncover relatively few instances of human rights violations and closed surveys can lead to 'forced' responses that may not reflect the complex reality of human rights conditions within the particular context in which the analysis is being carried out. For violations measurement work that uses surveys, the main challenge, which has begun to be met by Physicians for Human Rights, is to find ways of identifying likely samples of respondents for whom violations will be typical and then limiting the inferences that are drawn to the larger population of similar people. For general perceptions of human rights, the challenge is to devise questions and survey instruments in ways that capture meaningful understandings of human rights among mass publics.

Socio-economic and administrative statistics have traditionally not been used as measures for human rights and have typically been used by economists and development practitioners to analyse the economic progress of countries. The turn towards governance (see Weiss 2000; Landman and Häusermann 2003) in the late 1970s and early 1980s within international financial institutions (IFIs) and the United Nations Development Programme (UNDP), however, has carried with it an interest in developing measures of governmental institutional performance which include attention to the rule of law, accountability, transparency, corruption, democracy and in certain instances, human rights. While some of the governance indicators simply use standard-based scales, such as Freedom House, other efforts have sought to use socio-economic and administrative statistics in ways that capture government inputs, processes and outcomes that have a direct bearing on human rights. The key challenges for this kind of work are twofold: (1) the development of indicators that closely match or capture the human rights aspect of government performance and (2) capture the dynamic nature of human rights conditions across the population of a country, including between-group differences, and time-series changes.

Too often, analysts have used development indicators as human rights indicators, but it is our view that such a move is unsatisfactory. The Human Development Index (HDI) and the Physical Quality of Life Index (PQLI) measure overall levels of well-being and capture such things as income, life expectancy and literacy, but they are aggregate measures of outcomes which can have numerous explanatory factors that account for their cross-national variation. It is, thus, paramount to move beyond aggregate measures of general well-being and outcome to consider the ways in which measures could map specific government activities that relate to the obligations to respect, protect and fulfil. Such a move requires careful thinking about the many ways that government policies can have an impact on the different categories of human rights and that capture the time-dependent nature of such policies. We are, however, equally aware of the significant pragmatic challenge that such a move represents, since many countries simply lack the resources and technical capacity to collect such data on a regular basis.

Policy lessons

Beyond these more academic concerns over concepts and methods, we believe the volume also contains a number of lessons for policy-makers and practitioners working within non-governmental, governmental and intergovernmental organizations. First, there is a real need to recognize that there are no simple solutions to the human rights measurement problem. The process of measurement itself is complicated and the categories of dimensions of human rights are complex and in many ways inter-related. The multi-dimensional and multi-faceted nature of human rights suggests that it is not possible to devise a 'human rights index' of the kind often demanded in the international donor community. Moreover, there are often trade-offs between certain categories of rights that suggest any attempt to aggregate rights performance will mask significant differences between and within countries in ways that undermine larger policy goals of improving human rights performance. Second, as we showed in Chapter 3, any project on human rights measurement needs to establish the reason for measuring; the content and priorities of the project; the types of baselines, benchmarks and comparators against which a country-level or sector-level project is formulated; the type of personnel involved in the project; the types of measures that will be used and for which categories and dimensions of human rights; and the ways in which the project engages with local, national and international stakeholders in communicating its purpose, content, process and findings.

Finally, human rights start at the ground level in the lived experiences of real people under a variety of social, economic, political and cultural conditions, and now, more than ever, there is a need to find methods for engaging at the grassroots level in order to respect the dignity of those individuals who suffer human rights violations of whatever kind. Those who have worked for truth commissions, such as statement takers, data coders, analysts and commissioners, have learned to respect and restore victim dignity (some also use the term 'survivor') in ways that allow war-torn or post-authoritarian countries to heal and move forward. The insights gained from working with thousands upon thousands of survivors of large-scale atrocities around the world ought to apply to human rights practitioners working on everyday forms of human rights abuse that have less salience than those uncovered in truth processes. The positive intent of the international community can often get lost in the over-reliance on externally derived measures of human rights and thus the lessons of this volume, particularly in Chapter 4 on events-based measures and in Chapter 6 on survey-based measures, are that human rights measures must remain sensitive to the individual people and their experiences, which the process of measurement is seeking to capture, and in some way bring about positive change. We must not lose sight of the fact that measurement is not an end in itself, but a tool with which to help people.

Summary

It is clear from this volume and the observations made in this chapter that much has been done and that much needs to be done in the field of human rights measurement. We believe that this volume demonstrates the value and utility for the continued development and refinement of human rights measures.

Table 8.1 Comparison of different human rights measures

Type of Measure	Description	Primary categories of human rights addressed	Primary dimensions of human rights addressed	Strengths	Challenges
Events-based	Count data on acts of violation	Personal integrity rights, such as extra-judicial killing, torture, sexual violence, detention	Respect and protect, which includes state and non-state actors	Validity Reliability Context-specific Can show discrimination and between-group differences Good for capturing large-scale violations	Require advanced statistical knowledge May not be suitable for comparative analysis Tend to be produced for periods of violence, conflict, occupation and/or authoritarian rule
Standards-based	Subjective scales coded from narrative accounts on human rights at the country level	Aggregate forms of personal integrity rights Some application to economic and social rights	Respect	Available for large number of countries Available for long time-series Good for comparative analysis and large empirical generalisations	Less validity and reliability than events-based measures Variance truncation Source biases Making coding more transparent
Survey-based	Individual level measures of perceptions and experiences	Civil, political, and cultural, but can be easily applied to economic and social	Respect, but can easily be applied to protect and fulfil	Random samples Good for making inferences to target population Control over questions	Low strike rates Forced responses
Socio-economic and administrative statistics	Statistics on aspects of government performance and social demographics	Economic and social but can be applied to civil and political	Fulfil, but can be used to capture respect and protect	Objective Country level collection Discrete performance indicators	Sample sizes Disaggregation Indirect measures of rights National capacity for collection Government control over information

Demand for measures continues to rise and we have shown that there have been and are many ongoing efforts to satisfy this demand. Table 8.1 summarizes the main types of measures that have been outlined in this volume, including a general description of the measures, the primary categories of human rights that they capture (and their ability to expand to include other human rights), the primary dimensions of human rights that they measure (and their ability to expand to include additional dimensions), their relative strengths, and the remaining challenges that they need to confront in order to fill the gaps in their coverage and to respond to the general call for better measures of more aspects of human rights, which have hitherto existed. To that end, this volume has sought to synthesize the achievements in the field and set a path for the future development of human rights measurement. We do hope that with a careful reading of this volume, the measures that comprise much of the evidence about human rights can be improved, strengthened and made more widely available to the array of actors and stakeholders who are trying to make a difference for human rights around the world.

Further resources

2 The content of human rights

1 United Nations Office of the High Commissioner for Human Rights, www.ohchr.org
2 University of Minnesota Human Rights Library, www1.umn.edu/humanrts/index.html
3 Human Rights Education Associates (HREA), hrea.org
4 Human Rights Information and Documentation Systems, International (HURIDOCS), www.huridocs.org
5 Governance and Social Development Resource Centre, UK DFID database on human rights, www.gsdrc.org/go/topic-guides/human-rights

3 Measuring human rights

1 Benetech Human Rights Data Analysis Group (HRDAG), www.benetech.org/human_rights
2 Cingranelli and Richards Human Rights Data Project, www.humanrightsdata.com
3 Freedom House, www.freedomhouse.org
4 International IDEA State of Democracy Assessment (SOD), www.idea.int/sod/index.cfm
5 Political Terror Scale, www.politicalterrorscale.org
6 UNDP Oslo Governance Centre, www.undp.org/oslocentre
7 World Bank Governance Indicators Project, info.worldbank.org/governance/wgi/index.asp
8 World Values Survey, www.worldvaluessurvey.org

4 Events-based measures of human rights

1 Benetech Human Rights Data Analysis Group, www.benetech.org/human_rights/hrdag.shtml, www.hrdag.org/about/projects.shtml, www.hrdag.org/resources/Benetech-Report-to-CAVR.pdf
2 European Protest and Coercion Data, web.ku.edu/~ronfran/data/index.html
3 Kansas Events Data System (KEDS), web.ku.edu/~keds

5 Standards-based measures

1 Freedom House, www.freedomhouse.org
2 Cingranelli and Richards Human Rights Data Project, www.humanrightsdata.com
3 Political Terror Scale, www.politicalterrorscale.org
4 World Freedom Maps, freedom.indiemaps.com

6 Survey-based measures

1 Physicians for Human Rights, physiciansforhumanrights.org
2 Minorities at Risk, www.cidcm.umd.edu/mar
3 Minority Rights Group, www.minorityrights.org
4 www.dial.prd.fr
5 www.worldvaluessurvey.org

7 Socio-economic and administrative statistics

1 Center for Economic and Social Rights, www.cesr.org
2 Country Reports on Human Rights Practices, compiled by the US State Department Bureau of Democracy, Human Rights and Labor, www.state.gov
3 Human Rights Indicators at HURIDOCS, www.huridocs.org/tools/monitoring/indicators
4 Millennium Development Goals, www.un.org/millenniumgoals, www.undp.org/mdg
5 Penn World Tables, pwt.econ.upenn.edu
6 World Bank Data Bank, go.worldbank.org/SI5SSGAVZ0

Notes

2 The content of human rights

1 This conceptualization is similar to the 'measurement cycle' proposed by Adcock and Collier (2001: 531), who distinguish between the following: a) background concept, b) systematized concept, c) indicators and d) scores for cases. A background concept is 'the broad constellation of meanings and understandings associated with a given concept'. This background concept undergoes a process of conceptualization by a scholar or a group of scholars and is transformed into a systematized concept which is 'a specific formulation' of the background concept. The second level, i.e. measurement of the concept, begins when the systematized concept is operationalized into indicators. The indicators are used to score cases and the analysis of observed scores is, in turn, used to refine these indicators. The modified indicators can then assist in fine-tuning the systematized concept and provide insights into the meanings associated with the background concept.

2 On similar lines, the Special Rapporteur on the Right to the Highest Attainable Standard of Health suggests structural, process and outcome indicators to measure the right to health (Hunt 2006). Malhotra and Fasel (2005) reiterate this distinction by proposing two kinds of indicators: a) general indicators that measure the extent to which the process of implementing human rights includes the main human rights principles such as participation, inclusion, empowerment, non-discrimination and accountability; and b) indicators to measure the realization of substantive human rights.

3 Goertz (2006: 63–64) suggests that the concepts used at the indicator level should be in a substitutable relationship; being able to substitute indicators at this level of the concept allows greater flexibility, viability and opportunity to capture the local context and mechanisms used in research and measurement, without losing out on the validity of measures. However, this is not acceptable when applied to human rights as derived from international human rights law; human rights obligations require states to implement policies that ensure the enjoyment of rights while taking into consideration that the manner in which these policies are created and implemented does not violate human rights principles or standards (see CESCR 1999a, 1999b, 2000).

4 The two international human rights treaties, together with the UDHR, make up what is called the International Bill of Rights; this conception suggests that the protection and enjoyment of these rights is as important as fundamental rights enshrined in national constitutions (Freeman 2002; Nickel 2007).

5 The OHCHR Draft Guidelines on Poverty Reduction (Hunt et al. 2002) include the following as human rights principles that should determine 'a human rights based approach' and underlie all efforts towards poverty reduction: accountability, universality, non-discrimination and equality, participatory decision-making processes and the interdependence of rights.

6 The General Comment on the Right to Health replaces the principle of adaptability with the principle of quality (CESCR 2000: para 12).

4 Events-based measures of human rights

1 While other units of analysis are possible, to date MSE has been applied to estimating the number of people killed during a particular period of conflict, occupation and/or authoritarian rule.
2 This method is also known as 'capture-tag-recapture', since it originally used samples of fish that were caught, tagged, released and then caught again. Scientists could use the ratio of the probability of a tagged fish being caught to the probability of it not being caught to make a statistical estimation about the whole population of fish.

6 Survey-based measures

1 See europa.eu.int/comm/public_opinion/archives/ceeb_en.htm
2 Todd Landman visited Bangladesh as part of a project funded by the UK Department for International Development in 2006 and had the opportunity to interview the head of the Bureau of Statistics.
3 This use of 3 percent is based only on comparable surveys, as the Eurobarometer documentation does not list margins of error *per se*, an inconvenient omission that nevertheless does not detract from the discussion included here.

7 Socio-economic and administrative statistics

1 An indicator is a distilled measure of a concept. It may not be able to capture or represent the totality of a concept, especially if such a concept is characterized by multiple complex elements and dimensions, which is often the case for concepts in the social sciences (Miles 1985; Green 2001; Landman and Häusermann 2003; UNDP 2004).

References

Abouharb, R. and Cingranelli, D. L. (2007) *Human Rights and Structural Adjustment: The Impact of the IMF and World Bank*, Cambridge: Cambridge University Press.

Adcock, R. and Collier, D. (2001) 'Measurement validity: A shared standard for qualitative and quantitative research', *The American Political Science Review*, 95(3): 529–46.

Alfredsson, G. and Eide, A. (1999) *The Universal Declaration of Human Rights: A Common Standard of Achievement*, The Hague/ Boston/ London: Martinus Nijhoff Publishers.

Alston, P. (ed.) (2005) *Non-State Actors and Human Rights*, The Collected Courses of the Academy of European Law, Oxford: Oxford University Press.

Amnesty International (2007) 'From burning buses to caveirões: the search for human security' London: Amnesty International, 2 May 2007; AMR 19/010/2007.

Anand, S. and Sen, A. (2003) 'Human development index: Methodology and measurement' in S. Fukuda-Parr and A. K. Shiva Kumar (eds) (2003) *Readings in Human Development*, New York and New Delhi: Oxford University Press.

Anderson, C. J., Paskeviciute, A., Sandovici, M. E. and Tverdova, Y. V. (2005) 'In the eye of the beholder? The foundations of subjective human rights conditions in East-Central Europe', *Comparative Political Studies*, 38: 771–98.

Andreassen, B. A. (2003) 'Development, capabilities, rights: What is new about the right to development and a rights approach to development?' in M. Bergsmo (ed.) *Human Rights and Criminal Justice for the Downtrodden: Essays in Honour of Asbjørn Eide*, Leiden/Boston: Martinus Nijhoff Publishers.

An-Na'im, A. A. (1999) 'The position of Islamic states regarding the Universal Declaration of Human Rights' in P. Baehr, C. Flinterman and M. Senders (eds) *Innovation and Inspiration: Fifty Years of the Universal Declaration of Human Rights*, Amsterdam: Royal Academy of Arts and Sciences.

Apodaca, C. (2007) 'Measuring the progressive realization of economic and social rights' in S. Hertel and L. Minkler (eds) *Economic Rights: Conceptual, Measurement, and Policy Issues,* Cambridge University Press.

Asher, J. (2004) *The Right to Health: A Resource Manual for NGOs*, London and Washington, DC: Commonwealth Medical Trust and AAAS Science and Human Rights Program. Online. Available HTTP: < www.huridocs.org/tools/monitoring/tools/rthealth.pdf > (accessed on 18 February 2009).

Backman, G., Hunt, P., Khosla, R., Jaramillo-Strouss, C., Fikre, B. M., Rumble, C., Pevalin, D., Páez, D. A., Pineda, M. A., Frisancho, A., Tarco, D., Motlagh, M., Farcasanu, D. and Vladescu, C. (2008) 'Health systems and the right to health: an assessment of 194 countries', *The Lancet*, 372(9655): 2047.

Baehr, P., Flinterman, C. and Senders, M. (eds) (1999) *Innovation and Inspiration: Fifty Years of the Universal Declaration of Human Rights*, Amsterdam: Royal Academy of Arts and Sciences.

Balakrishnan, R. and Elson, D. (2008) 'Auditing economic policy in the light of obligations on economic and social rights', *Essex Human Rights Review,* Special Issue 5 (1) on Human Rights Perspectives: What We Have Learnt So Far. Online. Available HTTP: < ehrr.org >.

Balakrishnan, R., Elson, D. and Patel, R. (2009) *Rethinking Macro Economic Strategies from a Human Rights Perspective (Why MES with Human Rights II)*. Online. Available HTTP: < ushrnetwork.org/files/ushrn/MES-II.pdf > (accessed on 14 March 2009).

Baldock, J. (2007) 'Social policy, social welfare, and the welfare state' in J. Baldock, N. Manning and S. Vickerstaff (eds) *Social Policy,* 3rd edn, Oxford: Oxford University Press.

Ball, P. (2000a) 'The Salvadoran Human Rights Commission: Data processing, data representation, and generating analytical reports' in P. B. Ball, H. F. Spirer and L. Spirer (eds) *Making the Case: Investigating Large Scale Human Rights Violations Using Information Systems and Data Analysis*, Washington, DC: American Association for the Advancement of Science.

——(2000b) 'The Guatemalan Commission for historical clarification: Generating analytical reports, inter-sample analysis' in P. B. Ball, H. F. Spirer and L. Spirer (eds) *Making the Case: Investigating Large Scale Human Rights Violations Using Information Systems and Data Analysis,* Washington, DC: American Association for the Advancement of Science.

Ball, P. and Asher, J. (2002) 'Statistics and Slobodan: Using data analysis and statistics in the war crimes tribunal of former President Milosevic', *Chance*, 15(4): 15–24.

Ball, P., Asher, J., Sulmont, D. and Manrique, D. (2003) *How many Peruvians have Died? An Estimate of the Total Number of Victims Killed or Disappeared in the Armed Internal Conflict between 1980 and 2000*, Washington, DC: American Association for the Advancement of Science.

Ball, P., Guberek, T., Guzmán, D., Hoover, A. and Lynch, M. (2008) *Assessing Claims of Declining Lethal Violence in Colombia*, Palo Alto, CA: Benetech Initiative. Available HTTP: < www.hrdag.org/resources/publications/CO-PN-CCJ-match-working-paper.pdf > (accessed 5 April 2009).

Ball, P., Kobrak, P. and Spirer, H. (1999) *State Violence in Guatemala 1960–1996: A Quantitative Reflection*, Washington, DC: American Association for the Advancement of Science.

Ball, P., Spirer, H. and Spirer, L. (2000) *Making the Case: Investigating Large Scale Human Rights Violations Using Information Systems and Data Analysis*, Washington, DC: American Association for the Advancement of Science.

Ball, P., Tabeau, E. and Verwimp, P. (2007) *The Bosnian Book of Dead: Assessment of the Database*. Full Report. HiCN Research Design Note 5. Online. Available HTTP: < www.idc.org.ba/presentation/content.htm > (accessed 5 April 2009).

Ballesteros, A., Restrepo, J. A., Spagat, M. and Vargas, J. F. (2007) *The Work of Amnesty International and Human Rights Watch: Evidence from Colombia*, Bogota: CERAC – Centro de Recursos para el Análisis de Conflictos. Online. Available HTTP: < www. cerac.org.co/pdf/CERAC_WP_4.pdf > (accessed 3 April 2009).

Banks, A. S. (1994) *Cross-Polity Time-series Data Archive*, Binghamton, NY: State University of New York at Binghamton.

Barsh, R. L. (1993) 'Measuring human rights: problems of methodology and purpose', *Human Rights Quarterly*, 15(1): 87–121.

Beetham, D. (1999) *Democracy and Human Rights*, Cambridge: Polity.

Beetham, D., Carvalho, E., Landman, T. and Weir, S. (2008) *Assessing the Quality of Democracy: A Practical Guide*, Stockholm: International IDEA.

Bishop, Y. M., Feinberg, S. E. and Holland, P. H. (1975) *Discrete Multivariate Analysis: Theory and Practice*, Cambridge, MA: MIT Press.

Boli, J., Loya, T. A. and Loftin, T. (1999) 'National participation in world-polity organization' in J. Boli and G. M. Thomas (eds) *Constructing World Culture: International Nongovernmental Organizations Since 1875*, Stanford, CA: Stanford University Press.

Boli-Bennett, J. (1976) *The Expansion of Nation-States, 1870–1970*, PhD dissertation, Department of Sociology, Stanford University.

Bollen, K. A. (1992) 'Political rights and political liberties in nations: An evaluation of rights measures, 1950 to 1984' in T. B. Jabine and R. P. Claude (eds) *Human Rights and Statistics: Getting the Record Straight*, Philadelphia: University of Pennsylvania Press.

——(1998) *Cross National Indicators of Liberal Democracy, 1950 to 1990*, Codebook, Chapel Hill, NC: University of North Carolina.

Booth, D. and Lucas, H. (2001) 'Desk study of good practice in the development of PRSP indicators and monitoring systems: Initial review of PRSP documentation', Report commissioned by DFID for the Strategic Partnership with Africa. Online. Available HTTP: < siteresources.worldbank.org/INTPAME/Resources/Pov-Mon-Systems/PRSPindicators&MonSystem_B-L.pdf > (accessed on 26 February 2009).

Boyce, S. (2005) 'What Kind of Indicators can best monitor the delivery of the Children's Strategy?', briefing paper prepared for OFMDFM by the Children's Legal Centre and Save the Children. Online. Available HTTP: < www.savethechildren.org.uk > (accessed on 9 March).

Brockett, C. (2005) *Political Movements and Violence in Central America*, Cambridge: Cambridge University Press.

Brownlie, I. (2003) *Principles of Public International Law*, 6th edn, Oxford: Oxford University Press.

Bryman, A. and Cramer, D. (1999) *Quantitative Data Analysis with SPSS: A Guide for Social Scientists*, London: Routledge.

Buckingham, A. and Saunders, P. (2004) *The Survey Methods Workbook: From Design to Analysis*, Cambridge and Malden: Polity.

Bueno de Mesquita, B., Downs, G. W., Smith, A. and Cherif, F. M. (2005) 'Thinking Inside the Box: A Closer Look at Democracy and Human Rights', *International Studies Quarterly*, 49: 439–57.

Burkhart, R. E. and Lewis-Beck, M. (1994) 'Comparative Democracy, the Economic Development Thesis', *American Political Science Review*, 88(4): 903–10.

Burnham, G., Lafta, R., Doocy, S. and Roberts, L. (2006) 'Mortality after the 2003 Invasion of Iraq: A cross-sectional cluster sample survey', *The Lancet*, 368(9545): 1421–28.

Cain, M., Claude, R. P. and Jabine, T. B. (1992) 'A guide to human rights data sources' in T. B. Jabine and R. P. Claude (eds) *Human Rights and Statistics: Getting the Record Straight*, Philadelphia: University of Pennsylvania Press.

Callaway, R. L. and Harrelson-Stephens, J. (2004) 'The path from trade to human rights: The democracy and development detour' in S. C. Carey and S. C. Poe (eds) *Understanding Human Rights Violations: New Systematic Studies*, Aldershot: Ashgate.

Cammack, P. (1997) *Capitalism and Democracy in the Third World: The Doctrine for Political Development*, London and Washington: Leicester University Press.

Carvalho, E. (2008) 'Measuring children's rights: An alternative approach', *International Journal of Children's Rights*, 16(4): 545.

Chao, A. and Tsay, P. K. (1998) 'A sample coverage approach to multiple systems estimation with application to census undercount', *Journal of the American Statistical Association*, 93 (441): 283–93.

Chapman, A. (1996) 'A "violations approach" for monitoring the International Covenant on Economic, Social and Cultural Rights', *Human Rights Quarterly*, 18(1): 23–66.

——(2007) 'The status of efforts to monitor economic, social, and cultural rights' in S. Hertel and L. Minkler (eds) *Economic Rights: Conceptual, Measurement, and Policy Issues*, Cambridge: Cambridge University Press.

Chapman, A. and Russell, S. (eds) (2002) *Core Obligations: Building a Framework for Economic, Social and Cultural Rights*, Antwerp/ Oxford/ New York: Intersentia.

Cingranelli, D. L. and Richards, D. (2007) 'Measuring government effort to respect economic and social human rights: A peer benchmark' in S. Hertel and L. Minkler (eds) *Economic Rights: Conceptual, Measurement, and Policy Issues*, Cambridge: Cambridge University Press.

Cioffi-Revilla, C. (1990) *The Scientific Measurement of International Conflict: Handbook of Datasets on Crises and Wars, 1495–1988 AD*, Boulder, CO: Lynne Rienner.

——(1991) 'The Long-range analysis of war', *Journal of Interdisciplinary History*, 21: 603–29.

——(1996) 'Origins and evolution of war and politics', *International Studies Quarterly*, 40:1–22.

——(1998) *Politics and Uncertainty: Theory, Models, and Applications*, Cambridge: Cambridge University Press.

Cioffi-Revilla, C. and Lai, D. (1995) 'War and politics in ancient China, 2700 B.C. to 722 B.C.: Measurement and comparative analysis', *The Journal of Conflict Resolution*, 39(3): 467–94.

Cioffi-Revilla, C. and Landman, T. (1999) 'The rise and fall of Maya city states in the ancient Meso-American System', *International Studies Quarterly*, 43: 559–98.

Clapham, A. (2006) *Human Rights Obligations of Non-State Actors*, Oxford: Oxford University Press.

Claude, R. P. (ed.) (1976) *Comparative Human Rights*, Baltimore and London: Johns Hopkins University Press.

Claude, R. P. and Jabine, T. B. (1992) 'Exploring human rights issues with statistics' in T. B. Jabine and R. P. Claude (eds) *Human Rights and Statistics: Getting the Record Straight*, Philadelphia: University of Pennsylvania Press.

Clayton, R. and Pontusson, J. (1998) 'Welfare state retrenchment revisited: Entitlement cuts, public sector restructuring, and inegalitarian trends in advanced capitalist societies', *World Politics*, 51(1): 67–98.

Cochran, C. L. and Malone, E. F. (1995) *Public Policy: Perspectives and Choices*, New York: McGraw-Hill, Inc.

Committee Against Torture and Other Cruel, Inhuman or Degrading Treatment or Punishment (CAT) (2005), 'Guidelines on the form and content of initial reports under Article 19 to be submitted by States Parties to the Convention against Torture', CAT/C/4/Rev.3. Online. Available HTTP: < www.unhchr.ch/tbs/doc.nsf/(Symbol)/ CAT.C.4.Rev.3.en > (accessed 23 February 2009).

Committee on Civil and Political Rights (CCPR) (1989) 'General Comment No. 18. Non-discrimination', 10/11/89. Online. Available HTTP: < www.unhchr.ch/tbs/doc. nsf/(Symbol)/3888b0541f8501c9c12563ed004b8d0e > (accessed 28 January 2009).
——(1996) 'General Comment No. 25. The right to participate in public affairs, voting rights and the right of equal access to public service (Art. 25)', 12/07/96, CCPR/C/ 21/Rev.1/Add.7. Online. Available HTTP: < www.unhchr.ch/tbs/doc.nsf/(Symbol)/ d0b7f023e8d6d9898025651e004bc0eb > (accessed 28 January 2009).
——(2001) 'Consolidated guidelines for State reports under the International Covenant on Civil and Political Rights' 26/02/2001, CCPR/C/66/GUI/Rev.2. Online. Available HTTP: < www.unhchr.ch/tbs/doc.nsf/(Symbol)/CCPR.C.66.GUI.Rev.2.en > (accessed 23 February 2009).
——(2004) 'General Comment No. 31 [80]. Nature of the general legal obligation imposed on States Parties to the Covenant', 25/05/2004, CCPR/C/21/Rev.1/Add.13. Online. Available HTTP: < www.unhchr.ch/tbs/doc.nsf/(Symbol)/CCPR.C.21.Rev.1. Add.13.en > (accessed 28 January 2009).
Committee on Economic, Social and Cultural Rights (CESCR) (1989) 'CESCR General Comment No. 1. Reporting by States Parties', 24/02/89, E/1989/22. Online. Available HTTP: < www.unhchr.ch/tbs/doc.nsf/(Symbol)/38e23a6ddd6c0f4dc12563ed0051cde7 > (accessed 23 February 2009).
——(1990) 'CESCR General Comment No. 3. The nature of States Parties obligations (Art. 2, par. 1)', 14/12/90, CESCR/E/1991/23. Online. Available HTTP: < www.unhchr. ch/tbs/doc.nsf/(Symbol)/94bdbaf59b43a424c12563ed0052b664 > (accessed 28 January 2009).
——(1999a) 'General Comment No. 12. The right to adequate food (Art. 11)', 12/05/ 99, CESCR/E/C.12/1999/5. Online. Available HTTP: < www.unhchr.ch/tbs/doc.nsf/ (Symbol)/3d02758c707031d58025677f003b73b9 > (accessed 28 January 2009).
——(1999b) 'General Comment No. 13. The right to education (Art. 13)', 08/12/99, CESCR/E/C.12/1999/10. Online. Available HTTP: < www.unhchr.ch/tbs/doc.nsf/ (Symbol)/ae1a0b126d068e868025683c003c8b3b > (accessed 28 January 2009).
——(2000) 'General Comment No. 14. The right to the highest attainable standard of health (Art. 12)', 11/08/00, CESCR/E/C.12/2000/4. Online. Available HTTP: < www. unhchr.ch/tbs/doc.nsf/(Symbol)/40d009901358b0e2c1256915005090be > (accessed 28 January 2009).
Committee on the Elimination of Discrimination against Women (CEDAW) (1989) 'General Recommendation No. 9: Statistical data concerning the situation of women' Eighth Session. Online. Available HTTP: < www.un.org/womenwatch/daw/cedaw/ recommendations/recomm.htm > (accessed 23 February 2009).
Committee on the Elimination of Racial Discrimination (CERD) (2000) 'General Guidelines regarding the form and contents of reports to be submitted by State Parties under Article 9, Paragraph 1, of the Convention' CERD/C/70/Rev.5. Online. Available HTTP: < www.unhchr.ch/tbs/doc.nsf/(Symbol)/CERD.C.70.Rev.5.en > (accessed 23 February 2009).
Committee on the Protection of the Rights of all Migrant Workers and members of their Families (CMW) (2008) 'Guidelines for periodic reports to be submitted by State Parties under Article 73 of the Convention', CMW/C/2008/1. Online. Available HTTP: < www2.ohchr.org/english/bodies/cmw/docs/CMW.C.2008.1_en.pdf > (accessed 23 February 2009).
Committee on the Rights of the Child (CRC) (1996)'General guidelines regarding the form and content of periodic reports to be submitted by State Parties under Article

44, Paragraph 1 (b), of the Convention', UN Doc CRC/C/58. Online. Available HTTP: < www.unhchr.ch/tbs/doc.nsf/(Symbol)/CRC.C.58.Rev.1.en > (accessed 23 February 2009).

——(2003) 'General Comment No. 5. General measures of implementation of the Convention on the Rights of the Child (arts. 4, 42 and 44, para. 6)', CRC/GC/2003/5. Online. Available HTTP: < www.unhchr.ch/tbs/doc.nsf/(symbol)/CRC.GC.2003.5.en > (accessed 28 January 2009).

Conte, A. (2004) 'Democratic and civil rights' in A. Conte, S. Davidson and R. Burchill (eds) *Defining Civil and Political Rights: The Jurisprudence of the United Nations Human Rights Committee,* Aldershot: Ashgate.

Coppedge, M. and Reinicke, W. (1988) 'A scale of polyarchy' in R. D. Gastil (ed.) *Freedom in the World: Political Rights and Civil Liberties 1987–1988,* New York: Freedom House.

——(1990) 'Measuring polyarchy', *Studies in Comparative International Development,* 25(1): 51–72.

——(1991) 'Measuring polyarchy' in A. Inkeles (ed.) *On Measuring Democracy: Its Consequences and Concomitants,* New Brunswick, NJ: Transaction.

Cross, F. B. (1999) 'The relevance of law in human rights protection', *International Review of Law and Economics,* 19(1): 87–98.

Dahl, R. (1971) *Polyarchy: Participation and Opposition,* New Haven: Yale University Press.

Davenport, C. (1995) 'Multi-dimensional threat perception and state repression', *American Journal of Political Science,* 39(3): 683–713.

——(1996) '"Constitutional promises" and repressive reality: A cross-national time-series investigation of why political and civil liberties are suppressed', *The Journal of Politics,* 58(3): 627–54.

Davenport, C. and Armstrong, D. A. (2004) 'Democracy and the violation of human rights: A statistical analysis from 1976 to 1996', *American Journal of Political Science,* 48 (3): 538–54.

Davidson, S. (1993) *Human Rights,* Buckingham: Open University Press.

de Beco, G. (2007) 'Measuring human rights: Underlying approach', *European Human Rights Law Review,* 3: 266–78.

Department for International Development, UK (DFID) (2006) 'Eliminating world poverty: Making governance work for the poor. white paper on international development'. Online. Available HTTP: < www.dfid.gov.uk/wp2006/default.asp > (accessed 26 February 2009).

Diamond, J. (2005) *Collapse: How Societies Choose to Fail or Succeed,* London: Viking.

Dixon, W. J. and Moon, B. E. (1986) 'The military burden and basic human-needs', *Journal of Conflict Resolution,* 30(4): 660–84.

Donnelly, J. (1986) 'International human rights: A regime analysis', *International Organization,* 40: 599–642.

——(1999) 'Non-Discrimination and sexual orientation: Making a place for sexual minorities in the global human rights regime' in P. Baehr, C. Flinterman and M. Senders (eds) *Innovation and Inspiration: Fifty Years of the Universal Declaration of Human Rights,* Amsterdam: Royal Academy of Arts and Sciences.

Donnelly, J. (1999) 'Democracy, development, and human rights', *Human Rights Quarterly,* 21(3): 608–32.

——(2003) *Universal Human Rights in Theory and Practice,* 2nd edn, Ithaca, NY: Cornell University Press.

——(2007a) 'The relative universality of human rights', *Human Rights Quarterly,* 29: 281–306.

——(2007b) 'The west and economic rights' in S. Hertel and L. Minkler (eds) *Economic Rights: Conceptual, Measurement, and Policy Issues,* Cambridge University Press.

Donnelly, J. and Howard, R. E. (1988) 'Assessing national human rights performance: A theoretical framework', *Human Rights Quarterly,* 10(2): 214–48.

Dueck, J. (1992) 'HURIDOCS standard formats as a tool in the documentation of human rights violations' in T. B. Jabine and R. P. Claude (eds) *Human Rights and Statistics: Getting the Record Straight,* Philadelphia: University of Pennsylvania Press.

Duff, E. and McCamant, J., with Morales, W. (1976) *Violence and Repression in Latin America,* New York: Marcel Dekker, Inc.

Eide, A. (1989) 'Realization of social and economic rights: The minimum threshold approach', *International Commission of Jurists Review,* 43: 40–52.

——(2001) 'Economic, social and cultural rights as human rights' in A. Eide, C. Krause and A. Rosas (eds) *Economic, Social and Cultural Rights: A Textbook,* 2nd edn, Dordrecht/ Boston/ London: Martinus Nijhoff Publishers.

Ennew, J. (1997) 'Monitoring children's rights: Indicators for children's rights project', Childwatch International. Online. Available HTTP: < child-abuse.com/childhouse/ childwatch/cwi/projects/indicators/monitoring/ind_mon_index.html > (accessed 9 March 2009).

Fein, H. (1995) 'More murder in the middle: Life integrity violations and democracy in the world', *Human Rights Quarterly,* 17(1): 170–91.

Fitzgibbon, R. H. (1967) 'Measuring democratic change in Latin America', *Journal of Politics,* 29: 129–66.

Food and Agriculture Organization of the United Nations (FAO) (2008) *The State of Food Insecurity in the World 2008: High Food Prices and Food Security – Threats and Opportunities,* Rome: FAO.

Foweraker, J. and Krznaric, R. (2003) 'Differentiating the democratic performance of the West', *European Journal of Political Research,* 42(3): 313–40.

Foweraker, J. and Landman, T. (1997) *Citizenship Rights and Social Movements: A Comparative and Statistical Analysis,* Oxford: Oxford University Press.

——(2000) *Citizenship Rights and Social Movements: A Comparative and Statistical Analysis,* paperback edn, Oxford: Oxford University Press.

Francisco, R. (2000) 'Why are collective conflicts "stable"?' in C. Davenport (ed.) *Paths to State Repression: Human Rights Violations and Contentious Politics,* Lanham, MD: Rowman and Littlefield.

——(2004a) 'After the massacre: Mobilization in the wake of harsh repression', *Mobilization,* 2(2): 107–26.

——(2004b) 'The dictator's dilemma' in C. Davenport, H. Johnston and C. Mueller (eds) *Repression and Mobilization,* Minneapolis, MN: University of Minnesota Press.

Freedman, L. P. (1999) 'Reflections on emerging frameworks of health and human rights' in J. M. Mann, S. Gruskin, M. A. Grodin and G. J. Annas (eds) *Health and Human Rights: A Reader,* New York and London: Routledge.

Freeman, M. (2002) *Human Rights: An Interdisciplinary Approach,* Cambridge, UK and Malden, MA: Polity.

Fukuda-Parr, S., Raworth, K. and Shiva Kumar, A. K. (2003) 'Using the HDI for policy analysis' in S. Fukuda-Parr and A. K. Shiva Kumar (eds) *Readings in Human Development,* New York and New Delhi: Oxford University Press.

Fundar – Centro de Análisis e Investigación, the International Budget Project, and International Human Rights Internship Program (2004) *Dignity Counts: A Guide to*

Using Budget Analysis to Advance Human Rights, Online. Available HTTP: < www. iie.org/IHRIP/Dignity_Counts.pdf > (accessed 15 March 2009).

Gastil, R. D. (1978) *Freedom in the World: Political Rights and Civil Liberties, 1978*, Boston: G. K. Hall.

——(1980) *Freedom in the World: Political Rights and Civil Liberties*, Westport, CT: Greenwood Press.

——(1988) *Freedom in the World: Political and Civil Liberties, 1986–1987*, New York: Freedom House.

——(1990) 'The comparative survey of freedom: Experiences and suggestions' *Studies in Comparative International Development*, 25: 25–50.

Gibney, M. and Dalton, M. (1996) 'The political terror scale' in D. Cingranelli, *Human Rights and Developing Countries*, Greenwich, CT: JAI Press.

Gibney, M., Dalton, M. and Vockell, M. (1992) 'USA refugee policy: A human rights analysis update', *Journal of Refugee Studies*, 5(1): 37–46.

Gibney, M. and Stohl, M. (1988) 'Human rights and US refugee policy' in M. Gibney (ed.) *Open Borders? Closed Societies? The Ethical and Political Issues*, Westport, CT: Greenwood Press.

Gibson, J. S. (1996) *Dictionary of International Human Rights Law*, Lanham, MD: Scarecrow Press.

Giffard, C. (2002) *Torture Reporting Handbook*, Colchester, UK: Human Rights Centre, University of Essex.

Giles, J. (2008) 'The forensic humanitarian', *New York Times Magazine*, 17 February 2008.

Goertz, G. (2006) *Social Science Concepts: A User's Guide*, Princeton and Oxford: Princeton University Press.

Goldstein, R. J. (1992) 'The limitations of using quantitative data in studying human rights abuses' in T. B. Jabine and R. P. Claude (eds) *Human Rights and Statistics: Getting the Record Straight*, Philadelphia: University of Pennsylvania Press.

González Peña, A. and Restrepo, J. A. (2006) 'Desmovilización de las AUC: Mayor Seguridad Humana?' *UN Periódico*, 97 (September).

Goodin, R. E., Headey, B., Muffels, R. and Dirven, H.-J. (2000) 'The real worlds of welfare capitalism' in C. Pierson and F. G. Castles (eds) *The Welfare State Reader*, Oxford and Malden: Polity.

Green, M. (2001) 'What we talk about when we talk about indicators: Current approaches to human rights measurement', *Human Rights Quarterly*, 23: 1062–97.

Greer, D. (1935) *The Incidence of Terror During the French Revolution: A Statistical Interpretation*, Cambridge: Harvard University Press.

Gruskin, S. and Tarantola, D. (2005) 'Health and human rights' in S. Gruskin, M. A. Grodin, G. J. Annas and S. P. Marks (eds) *Perspectives on Health and Human Rights*, New York and London: Routledge.

Gruskin, S., Grodin, M. A., Annas, G. J. and Marks, S. P. (eds) (2005) *Perspectives on Health and Human Rights*, New York and London: Routledge.

Gurr, T. R. (1969) 'A comparative study of civil strife' in H. D. Graham and T. R. Gurr (eds) *Violence in America: Historical and Comparative Perspectives*, New York: Signet.

——(1970) *Why Men Rebel*, Princeton, NJ: Princeton University Press.

Guzmán, D., Guberek, T., Hoover, A. and Ball, P. (2007) *Missing People in Casanare*, Palo Alto, CA: Human Rights Data Analysis Group. Palo Alto, CA: Benetech Initiative. Online. Available HTTP: < www.hrdag.org/resources/publications/casanare-missing-report.pdf > (accessed 4 April 2009).

Hafner-Burton, E. M. (2005) 'Right or robust? The sensitive nature of political repression in an era of globalization', *Journal of Peace Research*, 42(6): 679–98.

Hafner-Burton, E. M. and Tsutsui, K. (2005) 'Human rights practices in a globalizing world: The paradox of empty promises', *American Journal of Sociology*, 110(5): 1373–1411.

——(2007) 'Justice lost! The failure of international human rights law to matter where needed most', *Journal of Peace Research*, 44(4): 407–25.

Hafner-Burton, E. M., Tsutsui, K. and Meyer, J. W. (2008) 'International human rights law and the politics of legitimation: Repressive states and human rights treaties', *International Sociology*, 23(1): 115–41.

Hannum, H. (1998) 'The UDHR in national and international law', *Health and Human Rights: An International Journal*, 3(2): 144–59.

Hasenclever, A., Mayer, P. and Rittberger, V. (2000) 'Integrating theories of international regimes', *Review of International Studies*, 26(1): 3–33.

Hathaway, O. (2002) 'Do treaties make a difference? Human rights treaties and the problem of compliance', *Yale Law Journal*, 111: 1932–2042.

——(2003) 'The cost of commitment', *Stanford Law Review*, 55:1821–62.

——(2007) 'Why do countries commit to human rights treaties?', *Journal of Conflict Resolution*, 51(4): 588–621.

Hayner, P. B. (2002) *Unspeakable Truths: Facing the Challenge of Truth Commissions*, New York: Routledge.

Helliwell, J. F. (1994) 'Empirical linkages between democracy and economic growth', *British Journal of Political Science*, 24: 225–48.

Henderson, C. (1991) 'Conditions affecting the use of political repression', *Journal of Conflict Resolution*, 35(1): 120–42.

——(1993) 'Population pressures and political repression', *Social Science Quarterly*, 74: 322–33.

Higgins, R. (1999) 'The continuing universality of the Universal Declaration' in P. Baehr, C. Flinterman and M. Senders (eds) *Innovation and Inspiration: Fifty Years of the Universal Declaration of Human Rights*, Amsterdam: Royal Academy of Arts and Sciences.

Hofferbert, R. I. and Cingranelli, D. L. (1996) 'Democratic institutions and respect for human rights' in D. L. Cingranelli (ed.) *Human Rights and Developing Countries*, Vol. 4, Greenwich, Connecticut and London, England: Jai Press Inc.

Hofrenning, D. J. B. (1990) 'Human Rights and foreign aid: A comparison of the Reagan and Carter Administrations', *American Politics Research*, 18: 514–26.

Holmes, S. (1999) *The Cost of Rights: Why Liberty Depends on Taxes*, New York: W. W. Norton.

Hoover, A., Silva, R. Guberek, T. and Guzmán, D. (2009) 'The "Dirty War" Index and the Real World of Armed Conflict', analytical paper published by the Human Rights Data Analysis Group, Palo Alto, CA: Benetech Initiative (www.benetech.org).

Huckerby, J. and Rodley, N. (2009) 'Outlawing torture: The story of Amnesty International's efforts to shape the UN Convention against Torture' in D. R. Hurwitz, M. L. Satterthwaite and D. Ford (eds) *Human Rights Advocacy Stories*, New York: Thomson Reuters/Foundation Press.

Human Rights Watch (2005) *Chad: The Victims of Hissène Habré Still Awaiting Justice*, July, Vol. 17, No. 10(A), New York: Human Rights Watch.

——(2006) *Judge, Jury, and Executioner: Torture and Extrajudicial Killings by Bangladesh's Elite Security Force*, December, Vol 18, No. 16(C), New York: Human Rights

Watch. Online. Available HTTP: < www.hrw.org/en/reports/2006/12/13/judge-jury-and-executioner > (accessed on 4 April 2009).

——(2007). *World Report 2007*, New York: Human Rights Watch.

Hunt, P. (2003a) 'Report of the UN Special Rapporteur on the right to health', United Nations Commission on Human Rights, E/CN.4/2003/58. Online. Available HTTP: < www2.ohchr.org/english/issues/health/right/annual.htm > (accessed 4 February 2009).

——(2003b) 'Report of the UN Special Rapporteur on the right to health', United Nations General Assembly, A/58/427. Online. Available HTTP: < www2.ohchr.org/english/issues/health/right/annual.htm > (accessed 4 February 2009).

——(2004a) 'Report of the Special Rapporteur on the right of everyone to the enjoyment of the highest attainable standard of physical and mental health, Paul Hunt', United Nations General Assembly, UN Doc. A/59/422. Online. Available HTTP: < www2.ohchr.org/english/issues/health/right/annual.htm > (accessed 4 February 2009).

——(2004b) 'Report of the Special Rapporteur on the right of everyone to the enjoyment of the highest attainable standard of physical and mental health, Paul Hunt', United Nations Commission on Human Rights, UN Doc. E/CN.4/2004/49. Online. Available HTTP: < www2.ohchr.org/english/issues/health/right/annual.htm > (accessed 4 February 2009).

——(2005) 'Report of the Special Rapporteur on the right of everyone to the enjoyment of the highest attainable standard of physical and mental health, Paul Hunt', United Nations Commission on Human Rights, UN Doc. E/CN.4/2005/51. Online. Available HTTP: < www2.ohchr.org/english/issues/health/right/annual.htm > (accessed 4 February 2009).

——(2006) 'Report of the Special Rapporteur on the Right of Everyone to the Enjoyment of the Highest Attainable Standard of Physical and Mental Health Mr. Paul Hunt', United Nations Commission on Human Rights, UN Doc. E/CN.4/2006/48. Online. Available HTTP: < www2.ohchr.org/english/issues/health/right/annual.htm > (accessed 4 February 2009).

——(2007) 'Report of the Special Rapporteur on the Highest Attainable Standard of Health', United Nations General Assembly, UN Doc. A/62/214. Online. Available HTTP: < www2.ohchr.org/english/issues/health/right/annual.htm > (accessed 4 February 2009).

——(2008) Report of the Special Rapporteur on the right of everyone to the enjoyment of the highest attainable standard of physical and mental health, Paul Hunt, United Nations Human Rights Council, UN Doc. A/HRC/7/11. Online. Available HTTP: < www2.ohchr.org/english/issues/health/right/annual.htm > (accessed 4 February 2009).

Hunt, P., Osmani, S. and Nowak, M. (2002) *Draft Guidelines: A Human Rights Approach to Poverty Reduction Strategies*, Prepared for the Office of the High Commissioner of Human Rights, New York and Geneva: United Nations.

Ignatieff, M. (2001) *Human Rights as Politics and Idolatry*, Princeton, NJ: Princeton University Press.

Inglehart, R. (1997) *Modernization and Postmodernization*, Princeton, NJ: Princeton University Press.

Institute for Democracy in South Africa (Idasa) (2001) *Budgeting for Child Socio-economic Rights: Government Obligations and the Child's Right to Social Security and Education*, Children's Budget Unit, Budget Information Service, Idasa.

International Labour Organization (ILO) (2006) *Training Materials for a Global Alliance against Forced Labour*, Turin: International Training Centre of the ILO.

International Working Group for Disease Monitoring and Forecasting (1995a) 'Capture-recapture and multiple-record systems estimation I: History and theoretical development', *American Journal of Epidemiology*, 142 (10): 1047–58.

——(1995b) 'Capture-recapture and multiple-record systems estimation II: applications in human diseases', *American Journal of Epidemiology*, 142 (10): 1059–77.

Jabine, T. B. and Claude, R. P. (eds) (1992) *Human Rights and Statistics: Getting the Record Straight*, Philadelphia: University of Pennsylvania Press.

Jaggers, K. and Gurr, T. R. (1995) 'Tracking democracy's third wave with the Polity III data', *Journal of Peace Research*, 32(4): 469–82.

Jahan, S. (2003) 'Evolution of the Human Development Index' in S. Fukuda-Parr and A. K. Shiva Kumar (eds) *Readings in Human Development*, New York and New Delhi: Oxford University Press.

Johnson, K. F. (1976) 'Scholarly images of Latin American political democracy in 1975', *Latin American Research Review*, 11(2):129–40.

——(1977) 'Research perspectives on the revised Fitzgibbon-Johnson index of the image of political democracy in Latin America, 1945–79', J. A. Wilkie and K. Ruddle (eds) *Quantitative Latin American Studies*, Statistical Abstract of Latin America, Los Angeles: UCLA.

——(1981) 'The 1980 image-index survey of Latin American political democracy', *Latin American Research Review*, 16: 193–201.

Johnson, N. F., Spagat, M., Gourley, S., Onnela, J-P. and Reinert, G. (2008) 'Bias in epidemiological studies of conflict mortality', *Journal of Peace Research*, 45 (5): 653–63.

Kaase, M. and Newton, K. (1995) *Beliefs in Government*, New York: Oxford University Press.

Kalyvas, S. N. (2006) *The Logic of Violence in Civil War*, Cambridge: Cambridge University Press.

Kaufmann, D., Kraay, A. and Zoido-Lobaton, P. (1999a) 'Aggregating governance indicators', *Policy Research Working Paper No. 2195*, Washington, DC: The World Bank.

——(1999b) 'Governance matters', *Policy Research Working Paper No. 2196*, Washington, DC: The World Bank.

——(2000) 'Governance matters: From measurement to action', *Finance and Development*, 37(2): 10–12.

——(2002) 'Governance matters II: Updated indicators for 2000–2001', *Policy Research Working Paper No. 2772*, Washington, DC: The World Bank.

Keck, M. and Sikkink, K. (1998) 'Transnational advocacy networks in the movement society' in D. S. Meyer and S. Tarrow (eds) *The Social Movement Society: Contentious Politics for a New Century*, Lanham, MD: Rowman & Littlefield.

Keith, L. C. (1999a) 'The United Nations International Covenant on Civil and Political Rights: Does it make a difference in human rights behavior?', *Journal of Peace Research*, 36(1): 95–118.

Keith, L. C. (1999b) 'Constitutional provisions for individual human rights (1976–96): Are they more than mere "window dressing"?', *Political Research Quarterly*, 55: 111–43.

Kimenyi, M. S. (2007) 'Economic rights, human development effort, and institutions' in S. Hertel and L. Minkler (eds) *Economic Rights: Conceptual, Measurement, and Policy Issues*, Cambridge: Cambridge University Press.

Knack, S. (2002) *Governance and Growth: Measurement and Evidence*, Forum Series on the Role of Institutions in Promoting Growth, Washington, DC: IRIS Center and USAID.

Koopmans, R. (1996) 'New social movements and changes in political participation in Western Europe', *West European Politics,* 19(1): 28–50.

Kritz, N. J. (ed.) (1995) *Transitional Justice: How Emerging Democracies Reckon with Former Regimes,* Washington, DC: United States Institute of Peace Press.

Kuhn, T. (1962) *The Structure of Scientific Revolutions,* Chicago: University of Chicago Press.

Kulas, J. (2008) *SPSS Essentials: Managing and Analyzing Social Sciences Data,* John Wiley and Sons.

Künnemann, R. and Epal-Ratjen, S. (2004) *The Right to Food: A Resource Manual for NGOs,* Washington, DC: AAAS Science and Human Rights Program and HURIDOCS. Online. Available HTTP: < www.huridocs.org/tools/monitoring/tools/rtfood.pdf > (accessed on 18 February 2009).

Landman, T. (2000) *Issues and Methods in Comparative Politics: An Introduction,* London: Routledge.

——(2002) 'Comparative politics and human rights', *Human Rights Quarterly,* 24(4): 890–923.

——(2003) *Issues and Methods in Comparative Politics: An Introduction,* 2nd edn, London: Routledge.

——(2004) 'Measuring human rights: Principle, practice and policy', *Human Rights Quarterly,* 26: 906–31.

——(2005a) *Protecting Human Rights: A Comparative Study,* Washington, DC: Georgetown University Press.

——(2005b) 'Review article: The political science of human rights', *British Journal of Political Science,* 35(3): 549–72.

——(2006a) *Studying Human Rights,* London and New York: Routledge.

——(2006b) *Human Rights and Social Exclusion Indicators: Concepts, Best Practices, and Methods for Implementation,* report prepared for the UK Department for International Development (DFID), on file with authors.

——(2008) *Issues and Methods in Comparative Politics: An Introduction,* 3rd edn, London: Routledge.

——(2009) 'Measuring human rights' in M. Goodhart (ed.) *Human Rights: Politics and Practice,* Oxford: Oxford University Press.

Landman, T. and Häusermann, J. (2003) *Map-Making and Analysis of the Main International Initiatives on Developing Indicators on Democracy and Good Governance,* University of Essex – Human Rights Centre and EUROSTAT.

Landman, T. and Larizza, M. (2009) 'Inequality and human rights: Who controls what, when, and how', *International Studies Quarterly* 53(3): 535–57.

La Porte, R., Yip, P. S. F., Bruno, G., Tajlma, N., Seben, G. A. F., Buddand, S. T., Cormack, R. M, Unwin, N., Chang, Y.-F., Fienberg, S. E., Junker, B. W., Libman, I. M. and McCarty, D. J. (1995) 'Capture-Recapture and Multiple-Record Systems Estimation I: History and Theoretical Development', *American Journal of Epidemiology,* 142 (10): 1047–1158.

Lasswell, H. D. (1951) *Politics: Who Gets What, When, and How,* Glencoe, IL: Free Press.

Lauren, P. G. (1998) *The Evolution of International Human Rights: Visions Seen,* Philadelphia: University of Pennsylvania Press.

Lipset, S. M. (1959) 'Some social requisites from democracy: Economic development and political legitimacy', *The American Political Science Review,* 53: 69–105.

Lynn, P. (2003) 'Development of a sampling method for household surveys in post-war Bosnia and Herzegovina', *ISER Working Paper No. 2003–26,* Colchester: ISER.

Online. Available HTTP: < www.iser.essex.ac.uk/publications/working-papers/iser/2003–26.pdf > (accessed 4 April 2009).

Macintyre, A. (1971) 'Is a science of comparative politics possible?' in A. Macintyre, *Against the Self-Images of the Age,* London: Duckworth.

Malanczuk, P. (1997) *Akehurst's Modern Introduction to International Law,* 7th revised edn, London: Routledge.

Malhotra, R. and Fasel, N. (2005) 'Quantitative human rights indicators: A survey of major initiatives', paper presented at the Nordic Network Seminar in Human Rights Research, 10–13 March, 2005, Abo, Finland.

Mann, J. M. (1999) 'Medicine and public health, ethics and human rights' in J. M. Mann, S. Gruskin, M. A. Grodin and G. J. Annas (eds) *Health and Human Rights: A Reader,* New York and London: Routledge.

Mann, J. M., Gruskin, S., Grodin, M. A. and Annas, G. J. (eds) (1999) *Health and Human Rights: A Reader,* New York and London: Routledge.

Mayer, L. C. (1989) *Redefining Comparative Politics: Promise versus Performance,* Newbury Park, CA: Sage.

Mazariegos, O. (2000) 'The International Center for Human Rights Investigations: Generating analytical reports' in P. Ball, H. Spirer and L. Spirer (eds) *Making the Case: Investigating Large Scale Human Rights Violations Using Information Systems and Data Analysis,* Washington, DC: American Association for the Advancement of Science.

McCamant, J. F. (1981) 'Social science and human rights', *International Organization,* 35(3): 531–52.

Meyer, W. (1996) 'Human rights and MNCs: Theory versus quantitative analysis', *Human Rights Quarterly,* 18(2): 368–97.

——(1998) *Human Rights and International Political Economy in Third World Nations,* London: Praeger.

Meyer, W. (1999a) 'Confirming, infirming, and "falsifying" theories of human rights: Reflections on Smith, Bolyard, and Ippolito through the lens of Lakatos', *Human Rights Quarterly,* 21(1): 220–28.

Meyer, W. (1999b) 'Human rights and international political economy in third world nations: Multinational corporations, foreign aid, and repression', *Human Rights Quarterly,* 21(3): 824–30.

Miles, I. (1985) *Social Indicators for Human Development,* London: Frances Pinter.

Milner, W. T., Leblang, D., Poe, S. C. and Smith, K. (2004) 'Providing subsistence rights: Do states make a difference?' in S. C. Carey and S. C. Poe (eds) *Understanding Human Rights Violations: New Systematic Studies,* Aldershot: Ashgate.

Milner, W. T., Poe, S. C. and Leblang, D. (1999) 'Security rights, subsistence rights, and liberties: A theoretical survey of empirical landscape', Human Rights Quarterly, 21(2): 403–43.

Mitchell, C., Stohl, M., Carleton, D. and Lopez, G. (1986) 'State terrorism: Issues of concept and measurement' in M. Stohl and G. Lopez (eds) *Government Violence and Repression: An Agenda for Research,* New York: Greenwood Press.

Mitchell, R. (2004) 'Quantitative analysis in international environmental politics: toward a theory of relative effectiveness' in A. Underdal and O. Young (eds) *Regime Consequences: Methodological Challenges and Research Strategies,* Cambridge: Cambridge University Press.

Mitchell, N. (2004) *Agents of Atrocity: Leaders, Followers, and the Violation of Human Rights in Civil War,* London: Palgrave.

Mitchell, N. and McCormick, J. M. (1988) 'Economic and political explanations of human rights violations', *World Politics*, 40: 476–98.

Mokhiber, C. G. (2005) 'Toward a measure of dignity: indicators for rights-based development' in S. Gruskin, M. A. Grodin, G. J. Annas and S. P. Marks (eds) *Perspectives on Health and Human Rights,* New York and London: Routledge.

Montgomery, J. D. (1999) 'Fifty years of human rights: An emergent global regime', *Policy Sciences*, 32(1): 79–93.

Moon, B. and Dixon, W. (1985) 'Politics, the state, and basic human needs: A cross-national study', *American Journal of Political Science,* 29(4): 661–94.

——(1992) 'Basic needs and growth-welfare trade-offs', *International Studies Quarterly,* 36(2): 191–212.

Moore, W. (2006) 'Synthesis v. Purity and Large-N Studies: How might we assess the gap between promise and performance?' *Human Rights and Human Welfare,* 6: 89–97.

Moravcsik, A. (2000) 'The origins of human rights regimes: Democratic delegation in postwar Europe', *International Organization*, 54 (Spring): 217–52.

Morsink, J. (1999) *The Universal Declaration of Human Rights: Origins, Drafting & Intent*, Philadelphia: University of Pennsylvania Press.

Muller, E. N. and Seligson, M. A. (1987) 'Inequality and insurgency', *American Political Science Review,* 81(2): 425–51.

Munck, G. and Verkuilen, J. (2002) 'Conceptualizing and measuring democracy: evaluating alternative indices', *Comparative Political Studies*, 35: 5–34.

Nankani, G., Page, J. and Judge, L. (2005) 'Human rights and poverty reduction strategies: Moving towards convergence' in P. Alston and M. Robinson (eds) *Human Rights and Development: Towards Mutual Reinforcement,* Oxford and New York: Oxford University Press and Center for Human Rights and Global Justice, New York University School of Law.

Neumayer, E. (2005) 'Do international human rights treaties improve respect for human rights?', *Journal of Conflict Resolution*, 49(6): 925–53.

Nickel, J. W. (2006) 'Human Rights', *Stanford Encyclopedia of Philosophy.* Online Available HTTP: < plato.stanford.edu/entries/rights-human > (accessed 10 December 2008).

——(2007) *Making Sense of Human Rights*, 2nd edn, Malden, Oxford and Victoria: Blackwell Publishing.

Norton, A. and Elson, D. (2002) 'What's behind the budget? Politics, rights and account-ability in the budget process', Overseas Development Institute. Online. Available HTTP: < www.odi.org.uk/rights/Publications/budget.pdf > (accessed 4 March 2009).

Nowak, M. (2003) *Introduction to the International Human Rights Regime*, The Raoul Wallenberg Institute Human Rights Library, Volume 14, Leiden/Boston: Martinus Nijhoff Publishers.

O'Sullivan, G. (2000) 'The South African Truth and Reconciliation Commission: Data-base representation' in P. B. Ball, H. F. Spirer and L. Spirer (eds) *Making the Case: Investigating Large Scale Human Rights Violations Using Information Systems and Data Analysis,* Washington, DC: American Association for the Advancement of Science.

Payne, L. (2000) *Uncivil Movements: The Armed Right Wing and Democracy in Latin America*, Baltimore: Johns Hopkins University Press.

Peterson, C. G. J. (1896) 'The yearly immigration of young plaice into the Limfjord from the German Sea', *Report of the Danish Biological Station to the Ministry of Fisheries*, 6: 1–48.

Physicians for Human Rights (1998) *The Taliban's War on Women: A Health and Human Rights Crisis in Afghanistan*, Boston, MA and Washington, DC: Physicians for Human Rights.

——(2002) *War-related Sexual Violence in Sierra Leone: A Population-based Assessment*, Boston, MA and Washington, DC: Physicians for Human Rights.

——(2007) *Epidemic of Inequality: Women's Rights and HIV?AIDS in Botswana & Swaziland*, Boston, MA and Washington, DC: Physicians for Human Rights.

Pickvance, C. (2007) 'The impact of social policy' in J. Baldock, N. Manning and S. Vickerstaff (eds) *Social Policy,* 3rd edn, Oxford: Oxford University Press.

Piron, L.-H. and Watkins, F. (2004) 'DFID human rights review: A review of how DFID has integrated human rights into its work', Overseas Development Institute, report prepared for the Department for International Development (DFID). Online. Available HTTP: < www.gsdrc.org/go/display/document/legacyid/1273 > (accessed 26 February 2009).

Poe, S. (1991) 'Human rights and the allocation of US military assistance', *Journal of Peace Research*, 28(2): 205–16.

——(1992) 'Human rights and economic aid allocation under Ronald Reagan and Jimmy Carter', *American Journal of Political Science*, 36(1): 147–67.

Poe, S. and Sirirangsi, R. (1993) 'Human rights and U.S. economic aid to Africa', *International Interactions*, 18(4): 1–14.

——(1994) 'Human rights and U.S. economic aid during the Reagan years', *Social Science Quarterly,* 75: 494–509.

Poe, S. and Tate, C. N. (1994) 'Repression of human rights to personal integrity in the 1980s: A global analysis', *American Political Science Review*, 88: 853–72.

Poe, S., Tate, C. N. and Keith, L. C. (1999) 'Repression of the human right to personal integrity revisited: A global cross-national study covering the years 1976–93', *International Studies Quarterly*, 43: 291–313.

Pritchard, K. (1986) 'Comparative human rights: An integrative explanation', *Politikon: South African Journal of Political Science*, 13(2): 24–37.

Raworth, K., (2001) 'Measuring human rights', *Ethics & International Affairs*, 15(1), 111–31.

Raworth, K. and Stewart, D. (2003) 'Critiques of the Human Development Index: A review' in S. Fukuda-Parr and A. K. Shiva Kumar (eds) *Readings in Human Development*, New York and New Delhi: Oxford University Press.

Restrepo, J., Spagat, M. and Vargas, J. F. (2006) 'Severity of the Colombian conflict: Cross-country data sets versus new micro data', *Journal of Peace Research*, 43 (1): 99–115.

Rich, R. (2002) 'Solidarity rights give way to solidifying rights', Research Paper, Centre for Democratic Institutions.

Richards, D. (2006) 'What do citizens mean when they say "Human Rights"? A comparative examination of the formation of citizen attitudes about, and understandings of, human rights', paper presented at the 2006 Annual Meeting of the American Political Science Association, Philadelphia, PA, 30 August–3 September.

Rights-based Municipal Assessment and Planning (RMAP) (2004) *Methodology and Tools for Human-Rights Based Assessment & Analysis, 2004*, UNDP and OHCHR.

Risse, T., Ropp, S. C. and Sikkink, K. (eds) (1999) *The Power of Human Rights: International Norms and Domestic Change*, Cambridge: Cambridge University Press.

Robinson, M. (2005) 'What rights can add to good development practice' in P. Alston and M. Robinson (eds) *Human Rights and Development: Towards Mutual Reinforcement,*

Oxford and New York: Oxford University Press and Center for Human rights and Global Justice, New York University School of Law.

Rodley, N. S. (2003) 'United Nations human rights treaty bodies and special procedures of the Commission on Human Rights – complementarity or competition?', *Human Rights Quarterly*, 25(4): 882–908.

Rosas, A. and Scheinin, M. (2001) 'Implementation mechanisms and remedies' in A. Eide, C. Krause and A. Rosas, (eds) *Economic, Social and Cultural Rights: A Textbook*, 2nd edn, Dordrecht/ Boston/ London, Martinus Nijhoff Publishers.

Rosenblum, J. (2004) *Monitoring Labor Rights: A Resource Manual for NGOs*, Washington, DC: AAAS Science and Human Rights Program and HURIDOCS. Online. Available HTTP: < www.huridocs.org/tools/monitoring/tools/rtlabour.pdf > (accessed 18 February 2009).

Rubin, B. R. and Newberg, P. R. (1980) 'Statistical analysis for implementing human rights policy' in P. R. Newberg (ed.) *The Politics of Human Rights*, New York: New York Press.

Ryan, J. E. (1994) 'Survey methodology', *Freedom Review*, 25(1): 9–13.

Samuelson, D. A. and Spirer, H. F. (1992) 'Use of incomplete and distorted data in inference about human rights violations' in T. B. Jabine and R. P. Claude (eds) *Human Rights and Statistics: Getting the Record Straight*, Philadelphia: University of Pennsylvania Press.

Sartori, G. (1970) 'Concept misinformation in comparative politics', *American Political Science Review*, 64: 1033–53.

Seltzer, W. and Anderson, M. (2008) 'Using population data systems to target vulnerable population subgroups and individuals: Issues and incidents' in J. Asher, D. Banks and F. J. Scheuren (eds) *Statistical Methods for Human Rights*, New York: Springer.

Sengupta, A. (2003) 'Development cooperation and the right to development' in M. Bergsmo (ed.) *Human Rights and Criminal Justice for the Downtrodden: Essays in Honour of Asbjørn Eide*, Leiden/Boston: Martinus Nijhoff Publishers.

Sepúlveda, M. (2003) *The Nature of the Obligations under the International Covenant on Economic, Social and Cultural Rights*, Antwerp/ Oxford/ New York: Intersentia.

Sherman, E. F. (1994) 'The US death penalty reservation to the International Covenant on Civil and Political Rights: Exposing the limits of the flexible system governing treaty formation', *Texas International Law Journal*, 29: 69–93.

Shrestha, B. and Oiron, O. (2006) 'Regional capacity building workshop on child rights based monitoring and evaluation tools and mechanisms', report prepared for Save the Children Sweden.

Shue, H., (1996) *Basic Rights*, 2nd edn, Princeton: Princeton University Press.

Silva, R. and Ball, P. (2006) *The Profile of Human Rights Violations in Timor-Leste, 1974–1999. A Report by the Benetech Human Rights Data Analysis Group to the Commission on Reception, Truth and Reconciliation of Timor-Leste*, Palo Alto, CA: Benetech Human Rights Data Analysis Group. Online. Available HTTP: < www.hrdag.org/resources/publications/Benetech-CAVR-statistical-report.pdf > (accessed 4th April 2009).

——(2007) 'The demography of conflict-related mortality in Timor-Leste (1974–99): Empirical quantitative measurement of civilian killings, disappearances & famine-related deaths' in J. Asher, D. Banks and F. J. Scheuren (eds) *Statistical Methods for Human Rights*, New York: Springer.

Simmons, B. A. (2000) 'International law and state behavior: commitment and compliance in international monetary affairs', *American Political Science Review*, 94(4): 819–35.

Skocpol, T. (1979) *States and Social Revolutions: A Comparative Analysis of France, Russia, and China*, Cambridge: Cambridge University Press.

Small, M. and Singer, J. D. (1983) *Resort to Arms: International and Civil Wars, 1816–1980*, Beverly Hills, CA: Sage.

Smith, J., Bolyard, M. and Ippolito, A. (1999) 'Human rights and the global economy: A response to Meyer', *Human Rights Quarterly*, 21(1): 207–19.

Spagat, M. and CERAC (2006) *Colombia's Paramilitary DDR: Quiet and Tentative Success*, Bogatá, Colombia: Centro de Recursos para el Análisis de Conflictos.

Spirer, H. F. and Seltzer, W. (2008) 'Obtaining evidence for the International Criminal Court using data and quantitative analysis' in J. Asher, D. Banks and F. J. Scheuren (eds) *Statistical Methods for Human Rights*, New York: Springer.

Steiner, H. J. and Alston, P. (1996) *International Human Rights in Context: Law, Politics, Morals. Text and Materials*, Oxford: Oxford University Press.

Stohl, M. and Carleton, D. (1985) 'The foreign policy of human rights: Rhetoric and reality from Jimmy Carter to Ronald Regan', *Human Rights Quarterly*, 7(2): 205–29.

Stohl, M., Carleton, D. and Johnson, S. (1984) 'Human rights and US foreign assistance from Nixon to Carter', *Journal of Peace Research*, 21(3): 215–26.

Stohl, M., Carleton, D., Lopez, G. and Samuels, S. (1986) 'State violations of human rights: issues and problems of measurement', *Human Rights Quarterly*, 8: 592–606.

Suesser, J. R. and Suarez de Miguel, R. (2008) 'Metagora: An experiment in the measurement of democratic governance' in J. Asher, D. Banks and F. J. Scheuren (eds) *Statistical Methods for Human Rights*, New York: Springer.

Suksi, M. (1993) *Bringing in the People: A Comparison of Constitutional Forms and Practices of the Referendum*, Dordrecht: Nijhoff.

Swedish International Development Cooperation Agency (Sida) (2003) *Digging Deeper: Four Reports on Democratic Governance in International Development Cooperation Summary*, Stockholm: Division for Democratic Governance, Sida.

——(2005) *Sida at Work: A Guide to Principles, Procedures and Working Methods*, Stockholm: Sida.

Symonides, J. (ed.) (2003) *Human Rights: International Protection, Monitoring, Enforcement*, Aldershot: Ashgate and UNESCO Publishing.

Tarrow, S. (1989) *Democracy and Disorder: Protest and Politics in Italy, 1965–1975*, Oxford: Clarendon Press.

Tashakkori, A. and Teddlie, C. (1998) *Mixed Methodology: Combining Qualitative and Quantitative Approaches*, London, Thousand Oaks and New Delhi: Sage Publications.

Taylor, C. and Hudson, M. (1972) *World Handbook of Political and Social Indicators*, 2nd edn, New Haven, CT: Yale University Press.

Taylor, C. and Jodice, D. A. (1983) *World Handbook of Political and Social Indicators: Political Protest and Government Change*, 3rd edn, New Haven, CT: Yale University Press.

Thompson, K. and Giffard, C. (2002) *Reporting Killings as Human Rights Violations*, Colchester, UK: Human Rights Centre, University of Essex.

Tilly, C. (1993) *European Revolutions, 1492–1992: The Making of Europe*, Oxford: Blackwell.

Tilly, C., Tilly, L. and Tilly, R. (1975) *The Rebellious Century 1830–1930*, Cambridge, MA: Harvard University Press.

Titmuss, R. (1968) 'Universalism versus selection' extract reproduced in C. Pierson and F. G. Castles (eds) (2000) *The Welfare State Reader*, Oxford and Malden: Polity Press.

ul Haq, M. (2003) 'The birth of the Human Development Index' in S. Fukuda-Parr and A. K. Shiva Kumar (eds) *Readings in Human Development,* New York and New Delhi: Oxford University Press.

United Nations (UN) (2006) 'Report on indicators for monitoring compliance with international human rights instruments', HRI/MC/2006/7, Eighteenth meeting of chairpersons of the human rights treaty bodies and Fifth inter-committee meeting of the human rights treaty bodies, Geneva. Online. Available HTTP: < www.unhchr.ch/ tbs/doc.nsf/0/c8603b9f3a39579ac1257186003898c2/$FILE/G0641960.pdf > (accessed 15 March 2009).

——(2008) 'Report on indicators for promoting and monitoring the implementation of human rights', HRI/MC/2008/3, Twentieth meeting of chairpersons of the human rights treaty bodies and Seventh inter-committee meeting of the human rights treaty bodies, Geneva. Available HTTP: < www2.ohchr.org/english/bodies/icm-mc/docs/ HRI.MC.2008.3EN.pdf > (accessed 15 March 2009).

United Nations Children's Fund (UNICEF) (2009) *The State of the World's Children 2009: Maternal and Newborn Health,* UNICEF.

United Nations Development Fund for Women (UNIFEM) (2008) *Progress of the World's Women 2005: Women, Work & Poverty,* UNIFEM.

United Nations Development Programme (UNDP) (1998) *Integrating Human Rights with Sustainable Human Development: A UNDP Policy Document,* New York: UNDP. Online. Available HTTP: < www.undp.org/governance/docs/HR_Pub_policy5.htm > (accessed 16 March 2009).

——(2000) *Human Development Report 2000,* New York/Oxford: Oxford University Press.

——(2002) *Handbook on Monitoring and Evaluating for Results,* New York: United Nations Development Programme Evaluation Office.

——(2004) *Governance Indicators: A Users' Guide,* New York: UNDP Oslo Governance Centre.

——(2006) *Indicators for Human Rights Based Approaches to Development in UNDP Programming: A User's Guide,* New York: UNDP.

United Nations Educational, Scientific and Cultural Organization (UNESCO) (2009) *Education for All Global Monitoring Report. Overcoming Inequality: Why Governance Matters,* UNESCO.

United Nations General Assembly (UNGA) (2005) 'In larger freedom: Towards development, security and human rights for all. Report of the Secretary General', UN Docs A/59/2005.

United Nations High Commissioner for Refugees (UNHCR) (2006) *The State of the World's Refugees: Human Displacement in the New Millennium,* UNHCR.

United States Agency for International Development (USAID) (1998) *Handbook of Democracy and Governance Program Indicators,* Washington, DC: Center for Democracy and Governance, Technical Publications Series, USAID. Online. Available HTTP: < www.usaid.gov/democracy/pubsindex.html > (accessed 16 March 2009).

United States Department of State (2007) *Country Practices on Human Rights: Brazil,* Washington, DC: The United States Department of State. (www.state.gov/g/drl/rls/ hrrpt/2006/78882.htm).

Van Bueren, G. (2002) 'The minimum core obligations of states under Article 10(3) of the International Covenant on Economic, Social and Cultural Rights' in A. Chapman and S. Russell (eds) *Core Obligations: Building a Framework for Economic, Social and Cultural Rights,* Antwerp/ Oxford/ New York: Intersentia.

Van Deth, J. (2009) 'Equivalence in Comparative Politics' in Todd Landman and Neil Robinson (eds) *The Sage Handbook of Comparative Politics*, London: Sage (forthcoming).

Vogt, W. P. (1999) *Dictionary of Statistics and Methodology: A Nontechnical Guide for the Social Sciences*, London: Sage.

Vreeland, J. R. (2008) 'Political institutions and human rights: Why dictatorships enter into the United Nations Convention against Torture', *International Organization*, 62 (01): 65–101.

Waltz, S. (2002) 'Reclaiming and rebuilding the history of the Universal Declaration of Human Rights', *Third World Quarterly*, 23(3): 437–48.

Ward, K. (2000) 'The United Nations Mission for the Verification of Human Rights in Guatemala: Database representation' in P. Ball, H. Spirer and L. Spirer (eds) *Making the Case: Investigating Large Scale Human Rights Violations Using Information Systems and Data Analysis*, Washington, DC: American Association for the Advancement of Science.

Wantchekon, L. and Healy, A. (1999) 'The "Game" of Torture', *Journal of Conflict Resolution*, 43(5), 596–609.

Weisberg, H. (2005) *The Total Survey Error Approach: A Guide to the New Science of Survey Research*, Chicago: University of Chicago Press.

Weiss, T. (2000) 'Governance, Good Governance and Global Governance: Conceptual and Actual Challenges', *Third World Quarterly*, 21(5): 795–814.

Whiteley, P. (1999) 'The origins of social capital' in J. Van Deth, M. Maraffi, K. Newton and P. Whiteley (eds) *Social Capital and European Democracy*, London: Routledge.

Whiteley, P. (2000) 'Economic growth and social capital', *Political Studies*, 48: 443–66.

Wickham-Crowley, T. (1993) *Guerillas and Revolution in Latin America*, Princeton, NJ: Princeton University Press.

Wilkie, J. A. and Ruddle, K. (1992), *Quantitative Latin American Studies*, Statistical Abstract of Latin America, Los Angeles: UCLA.

Wilson, R. A. (2001) *The Politics of Truth and Reconciliation in South Africa: Legitimizing the Post-Apartheid State*, Cambridge, Cambridge University Press.

Wolf, E. (1969) *Peasant Wars of the Twentieth Century*, New York: Harper and Row.

Womack, J. (1969) *Zapata and the Mexican Revolution*, New York: Knopf.

World Bank (2007) 'Country Policy and Institutional Assessments. 2007 assessment questionnaire'. Online. Available HTTP: < www1.worldbank.org/operations/IRAI/2007/CPIA07Criteria.pdf > (accessed 5 April 2009).

World Health Organization (WHO) (2008) *The World Health Report 2008. Primary Health Care: Now More than Ever*, WHO.

Zaller, J. and Feldman, S. (1992) 'A simple theory of survey response: Answering questions versus revealing preferences', *American Journal of Political Science*, 36: 579–616.

Zanger, S. C. (2000a) 'Good governance and European aid: The impact of political conditionality', *European Union Politics*, 1(3): 293–317.

Zanger, S. C. (2000b) 'A global analysis of the effect of regime change on life integrity violations, 1977–93', *Journal of Peace Research*, 37(2): 213–33.

Zeller, R. and Carmines, E. (1980) *Measurement in the Social Sciences: The Link between Theory and Data*, Cambridge: Cambridge University Press.

Zwane, E. and van der Heijden, P. (2005) 'Population estimation using the multiple system estimator in the presence of continuous variables', *Statistical Modelling*, 5: 39–52.

Index

Page numbers in bold indicate tables and figures.